Robert Frost

Selected Poems

Edited by Steven Croft

Oxford University Press

OXFORD

UNIVERSITY PRESS

Great Clarendon Street, Oxford OX2 6DP

Oxford University Press is a department of the University of Oxford.
It furthers the University's objective of excellence in research, scholarship,
and education by publishing worldwide in

Oxford   New York

Auckland   Cape Town   Dar es Salaam   Hong Kong   Karachi
Kuala Lumpur   Madrid   Melbourne   Mexico City   Nairobi
New Delhi   Shanghai   Taipei   Toronto

With offices in

Argentina   Austria   Brazil   Chile   Czech Republic   France   Greece
Guatemala   Hungary   Italy   Japan   South Korea   Poland   Portugal
Singapore   Switzerland   Thailand   Turkey   Ukraine   Vietnam

Oxford is a registered trade mark of Oxford University Press
in the UK and in certain other countries

British Library Cataloguing in Publication Data

Data available

ISBN: 978-0-19-8325710

3 5 7 9 10 8 6 4

Typeset in India by TNQ Books and Journals Pvt. Ltd.

Printed in China by Printplus

Paper used in the production of this book is a natural, recyclable product made from
wood grown in sustainable forests. The manufacturing process conforms to the environ-
mental regulations of the country of origin.

The publishers would like to thank the following for permission to reproduce photographs:

Page 4: Jeffrey M. Frank/Shutterstock; page 6: Getty Images; page 8: Bettmann/Corbis;
page 13: Bettmann/Corbis; page 116: Ron and Patty Thomas/Getty Images; page 118:
Marvin Koner/Corbis; page 121: Dennis Welsh/Photolibrary; page 131: Cardiff
University Library Archive; page 141: Bettmann/Corbis; page 150: Bettmann/Corbis.

Contents

Acknowledgements

The publishers and editors would like to thank Adrian Barlow for permission to reprint his Notes section in this new edition.

The text of the poems is from *The Poetry of Robert Frost*, edited by Edward Connery Lathem (Jonathan Cape, 1971), reprinted by permission of The Random House Group on behalf of the Estate of Robert Frost.

Acknowledgements from Steven Croft

I would like to thank Sandra Haigh for offering her interesting and, sometimes, contentious views on the poetry. I am also grateful to Jan Doorly for her helpful and constructive advice and sensitive editing of the manuscript.

Editors

Dr Victor Lee, the series editor, read English at University College, Cardiff. He was later awarded his doctorate at the University of Oxford. He has taught at secondary and tertiary level, working at the Open University for 27 years. Victor Lee's experience as an examiner is very wide. He has been, for example, a Chief Examiner in English A level for three different boards, stretching over a period of more than 30 years.

Steven Croft holds degrees from Leeds and Sheffield universities. He has taught at secondary and tertiary level and headed the Department of English and Humanities in a tertiary college. He has 25 years' examining experience at A level and is currently a Principal Examiner for English. He has written several books on teaching English at A level, and his publications for Oxford University Press include *Exploring Literature*, *Success in AQA Language and Literature* and *Exploring Language and Literature*. He is the series editor for many recent titles in the Oxford Student Texts series.

Foreword

Oxford Student Texts are specifically aimed at presenting poetry and drama to an audience studying English literature at an advanced level. Each text is designed as an integrated whole consisting of four main parts. The first part sets the scene by discussing the context in which the work was written. The most important part of the book is the poetry or play itself, and it is suggested that the student read this first without consulting the Notes or other secondary sources. To encourage students to follow this advice, the Notes are placed together after the text, not alongside it. Where help is needed, the Notes and Interpretations sections provide it.

The Notes perform two functions. First, they provide information and explain allusions. Second (this is where they differ from most texts at this level), they often raise questions of central concern to the interpretation of the poetry or play being dealt with, particularly in the general note placed at the beginning of each set of notes.

The fourth part, the Interpretations section, deals with major issues of response to the particular selection of poetry or drama. One of the major aims of this part of the text is to emphasize that there is no one right answer to interpretation, but a series of approaches. Readers are given guidance as to what counts as evidence, but in the end left to make up their own minds as to which are the most suitable interpretations, or to add their own.

In these revised editions, the Interpretations section now addresses a wider range of issues. There is a more detailed treatment of context and critical history, for example. The section contains a number of activity-discussion sequences, although it must be stressed that these are optional. Significant issues about the poetry or play are raised, and readers are invited to tackle activities before proceeding to the discussion section, where possible responses to the questions raised are considered. Their main function is to engage readers actively in the ideas of the text.

At the end of each text there is also a list of Essay Questions. Whereas the activity-discussion sequences are aimed at increasing understanding of the literary work itself, these tasks are intended to help explore ideas about the poetry or play after the student has completed the reading of the work and the studying of the Notes and Interpretations. These tasks are particularly helpful for coursework projects or in preparing for an examination.

Victor Lee   *Series Editor*

Robert Frost in Context

Robert Frost has been lauded as one of the most successful – if not *the* most successful – of all American poets. His work attracted both popular and critical acclaim throughout his career. His poetry is often seen as being deeply rooted in the traditional American values of plain speaking, straightforwardness, and the practical self-reliance of a farmer poet who is inspired by the life of the farm and the natural world. This is an image that Frost did much to cultivate, but there is considerably more to both the man and his poetry than this view suggests.

In the years since his death in 1963, Frost's work has continued to receive the attention of the literary world while retaining its popularity with a much wider readership. The breadth of this appeal lies, to a large degree, in the fact that his poems take their starting points from the world around us, from nature and from universal aspects of human lives; the ideas and themes they explore are centred on experiences to which we can all relate. The apparent simplicity with which Frost presents his ideas has its own appeal, but the complexity that underpins his poetry means it can be read on many different levels.

Frost's early life

Although known primarily for his depictions of the rural life of New England, Frost was born on the west coast of the United States, in San Francisco, on 26 March 1874. He was named Robert Lee Frost, after the renowned Confederate general of the American Civil War, Robert E. Lee. Frost's father William had run away from his home in Massachusetts as a teenager to join the Confederate Army and had served under Lee briefly.

William Frost had married Isabelle Moodie in 1873 and both had worked for a time as schoolteachers in Pennsylvania before moving to San Francisco, where William Frost became city editor of the *San Francisco Evening Post*. He soon became involved in politics and resigned his job as editor in 1884 to stand for election, but lost twice. He suffered from depression and had already been diagnosed with tuberculosis; his health declined, hastened by heavy drinking. He died of tuberculosis in May 1885, leaving the family with little money. However, with the financial help of Frost's grandfather, William Frost Senior, Frost's mother moved the family across the country to Lawrence, Massachusetts, where she and her two children lived for a time with her husband's parents. Frost began school in Salem, where his mother had found a position as a teacher.

In 1888 Frost passed the entrance exam for Lawrence High School and enrolled there on a college prep programme. His studies followed the classical model and included Latin, Greek, and Roman and European history, as well as English literature. His academic ability soon became evident and his top grades showed that he was a student with a great deal of potential.

As well as developing his mind through study during this period, Frost broadened his life experience by taking on various kinds of casual work between 1885, when he arrived in New England, and 1892 when he left (briefly) to go to Dartmouth College. This work included general farm labouring and working in a woollen mill and a shoe factory. Many of his poems centre on a particular task that he did, such as the scything of the grass in *Mowing* and the apple picking in *After Apple-Picking*. It was also during this period that he developed an interest in natural history (particularly botany), astronomy, and theories of evolution. This interest in nature and the natural cycle lies at the heart of many of his poems.

In April 1890 his first published poem, *La Noche Triste*, appeared in the school magazine, *The Bulletin*, and more were to follow. He later became editor of the magazine and crowned his academic success at Lawrence High School by passing the entrance exam to Harvard College.

At this time he fell in love with Elinor White, a fellow student at Lawrence High School, and many of his earlier poems are written to, or are about, her. In 1892 they became secretly engaged.

On leaving high school, Frost did not go to Harvard as intended but was persuaded by his grandparents to go to Dartmouth College instead. His grandparents believed that the influences of student life at Harvard had been, at least in part, responsible for the habits that Frost's father had developed. However, Frost did not settle at Dartmouth and he left the college in December 1892 without completing his first semester. Although Dartmouth itself had little influence on Frost, he did discover while studying there a famous anthology of English poetry, Palgrave's *The Golden Treasury* (first published in 1861). The influence of this volume, as William H. Pritchard comments in his biography of Frost (see Further Reading page 157), 'lasted all his life' and 'helped to extend his taste back from the nineteenth century into earlier English poetry'.

After leaving Dartmouth, Frost had various jobs. He helped out with teaching his mother's class for a time, and later took a job in a local mill replacing the filaments in the lamps, spending his free time studying Shakespeare. He tried to persuade Elinor, who was studying at St Lawrence University in New York State, to leave college and marry him, but she refused and continued her studies. In 1894 he left his job at the mill and took up a teaching appointment in Salem, and at this time his poem *My Butterfly: An Elegy* was accepted by a magazine called *The Independent*, which paid him $15 for it.

When a further attempt to persuade Elinor to leave college and marry him failed, Frost left Salem in despair and travelled aimlessly to the area on the border between Virginia and North Carolina, aptly – given Frost's state of mind – named the 'Great Dismal Swamp'. He returned to Lawrence in November, and in December the following year he and Elinor were finally married.

Their first child, Elliott, was born in September 1896 and, with the idea of improving his qualifications to enable him to obtain a higher salary in teaching, Frost gained a place at Harvard and began his studies there in the autumn of 1897, supported

3

financially by his grandfather. He quickly achieved academic success here too, and in his first year he won a scholarship.

However, in March 1899, partly, at least, on the advice of his doctor who had recommended that outdoor work rather than academic study would benefit his health, Frost decided to leave Harvard and become a chicken farmer. Again with financial help from his grandfather, he bought a farm at Derry, New Hampshire and began a new career in farming. His daughter Lesley was born in December 1899, but tragedy quickly followed: Frost's mother was diagnosed with terminal cancer early in 1900 and in July his son Elliott died of cholera. Frost's mother died soon after.

During the period 1901 to 1906, Frost worked full time as a farmer but also continued to write poetry. In 1906 three poems, including *The Tuft of Flowers*, were accepted for publication, and it is likely that *Mowing* was also written during this period,

The farm in Derry, New Hampshire where the Frosts lived
from 1900 to 1911

although it was not published until his collection *A Boy's Will* appeared in 1913.

Busy as he was with the farm and his poetry, Frost's family life became more hectic too at this time as Elinor gave birth to a son, Carol, in 1902, and daughters Irma and Marjorie in 1903 and 1905. Another daughter, Elinor, was born in 1907 but died shortly after birth.

From 1906 Frost began to return to teaching, part time at first, and then full time by the end of the year, teaching English at Pinkerton Academy. He took charge of the English curriculum and devised a programme of study in English that was radical in its emphasis on the spoken word and the notion of reading for pleasure. Such was his success at Pinkerton that he was invited to speak at a convention of English teachers about his ideas and methods, and in 1911 was offered a position in a teacher training institution at Plymouth, which he accepted. The family moved to Plymouth where Frost taught psychology and education at the Plymouth State Normal School (now Plymouth State University) – a college for training young women teachers.

However, before long Frost's desire to devote more of his time to poetry brought further change, and he and Elinor felt they needed to make a new start somewhere else. They decided to sell the farm and move to England where, on the proceeds from the farm and the annuity left by his grandfather, they felt they could live for several years. Frost also hoped to be able to find a publisher for his poems there, while Elinor was attracted by the romantic notion of living 'under thatch'. The farm was sold in November 1911 and the Frosts prepared for the move.

Frost in England

On 23 August 1912 Frost and Elinor, with their children, sailed from Boston to Glasgow on the *S.S. Parisian*. On arrival they travelled to London where they found lodgings for a week before moving to a rented cottage at Beaconsfield, about 20 miles north-west of

London. Frost had brought with him many poems, which he intended to organize into volumes of poetry ready for publication. He prepared the manuscript for *A Boy's Will* – a collection of over 30 poems arranged by theme and imagery. He submitted the manuscript to David Nutt and Company, a London publisher, and it was accepted for publication. *A Boy's Will* was published in April 1913; Frost was 39.

Apart from the publication of his first volume of poetry, Frost's time in England also had other benefits as it gave him the opportunity to meet many significant figures in the literary society of England. He was introduced to his fellow American poet Ezra Pound – also living in England – who praised *A Boy's*

Robert Frost in England in 1913

Will in the influential magazine *Poetry*, although later the relationship between the two poets became strained. *A Boy's Will* received various other positive reviews, and Frost optimistically looked forward to building on this success in future collections.

Through his association with Pound, Frost also met various other influential poets and writers of the time, including T.E. Hulme, Ford Madox Ford, Rupert Brooke, Robert Graves and Walter de la Mare. One highly respected critic who had written a particularly favourable review of Frost's work was Edward Thomas, later to become a noted poet himself. The two had been introduced at a London teashop and they were soon to become friends. In 1914 Frost and his family moved to the village of Dymock in Gloucestershire, an area where several literary figures including Wilfrid Gibson and Lascelles Abercrombie lived. Edward Thomas and his family were frequent visitors there and a strong friendship developed between Frost and Thomas.

Four years younger than Frost, Thomas was a well-established and well-respected critic and reviewer, and had written a number of important critical and biographical studies. However, he felt the need to express himself in a more creative way and Frost persuaded him to begin writing poetry. The two had much in common in terms of both their personal lives and their ideas on poetry, and Frost has said that Thomas provided the inspiration for one of his most famous poems, *The Road Not Taken*. It has been said that 'Frost spoke of Thomas as if they were spiritual brothers', and he later wrote: 'I never had, I never shall have another such year of friendship'. It was a friendship that was to be cut short, however, when Thomas was killed in action during the Battle of Arras on 9 April 1917.

In May 1915 Frost's second volume of poetry, *North of Boston*, was published by David Nutt and received favourable reviews in a wide range of journals including *The Times Literary Supplement*, *Pall Mall Gazette*, *The English Review* and *The Daily News*. Once again Thomas's reviews were extremely positive, pointing to the essential quality of Frost's poems – notably the

Frost in 1916, in a photograph taken to publicize his second volume of poetry, *North of Boston*

use of the language of everyday life and the voice of authentic speech, rather than an attempt to create artificial poetic effects. Frost, like Thomas, believed that the relationship between speech, voice and form was of central importance to poetry.

Although Frost's literary reputation was greatly enhanced with the publication of *North of Boston*, by now his financial reserves were running low and he decided to return to America, a decision not entirely without risk. The First World War had begun in August 1914, and crossing the Atlantic at this time had an element of the unpredictable about it.

Return to America

Frost and his family sailed from Liverpool to New York on 13 February 1915. His two and a half years in England had made a difference; he had left America with aspirations to make his mark on the literary world and he was returning as a published poet with two volumes of poetry to his name that had attracted favourable reviews from respected literary figures. He was further pleased to find that his success in England had been noticed back home in America, and that *North of Boston* had received a generally favourable review by the American poet and writer Amy Lowell, who, like other reviewers, praised the simplicity and directness of his language and style.

Very soon after Frost's arrival back in the United States, the American publisher Henry Holt published *North of Boston* and *A Boy's Will*, soon prompting more favourable reviews. Frost bought a farm in Franconia, New Hampshire and the family settled there, although much of his time was taken up in giving talks and readings throughout New England. In November 1916 his third volume of poetry, *Mountain Interval*, was published. This collection contains two of his most famous poems, *The Road Not Taken* and *Birches*, which many have regarded as exploring significant and universal human experiences.

He accepted a teaching post for one semester at Amherst College, and at the beginning of 1917 moved to Amherst to take up the post there. This was also the year that brought the tragic news of the death of Edward Thomas, killed at the Battle of Arras. The post at Amherst, originally for one semester, was extended and Frost spent three years there. He resigned in February 1920 after a disagreement with the college president, Alexander Meiklejohn, but also wanted to devote more time to writing. The farm at Franconia was sold and the family moved from Amherst to Vermont, where Frost took up a position as consulting editor for Henry Holt and Company.

During this time his sister Jeanie had become mentally ill and Frost had to have her committed to the state mental hospital in

Augusta, Maine. In 1921 Frost accepted a fellowship at the University of Michigan, which he held for two years before returning to teach at Amherst. He also began his life-long association with the Bread Loaf School of English at Middlebury College in Ripton, Vermont.

In 1923 Frost published his *Selected Poems* followed by his fourth collection of poetry, *New Hampshire*, for which he was awarded a Pulitzer Prize and received an honorary doctorate from Middlebury College and Yale University.

Both books sold very well, and it was clear that Frost's reputation as a poet of some stature had grown considerably since his return to the United States, but the poems in *New Hampshire* marked a shift in his poetry. Some have commented that part of Frost's popularity had been created by the image that he had projected through his many public recitals and talks – he had perhaps, as he had commented in a letter to Louis Untermeyer in 1916, become his own salesman.

In 1924 he gave notice to Amherst College that he had accepted a lifetime appointment at the University of Michigan as Fellow in Letters, a position that held no teaching commitment. He took up the position in the autumn of 1925, leaving his family in New England. However, the ill health of both his daughters Marjorie and Irma put great strain on him and he felt that he was responsible for scattering the family. In view of this, he accepted an offer to return to Amherst College and began teaching there again for the winter, teaching special classes in English and holding 'informal conferences' with students.

Later years

In 1928 Frost signed a new contract with Holt and in the summer of that year, after the completion of his next volume of poetry, *West-Running Brook*, he decided to go to Europe with Elinor and

Marjorie. Marjorie was to stay with a family in France while her father and mother went on to England to see old friends. However, Frost was concerned about the health of Marjorie, whom they had brought in the hope that the trip would help her as well as Elinor, who was suffering from depression. Travelling through England and Scotland, Frost met many old friends, and was introduced to T.S. Eliot and Robert Bridges. Later, visiting Dublin, he met W.B. Yeats.

The Frosts returned to America in November. After *West-Running Brook* an expanded edition of *Selected Poems* was published, followed by *Collected Poems* in 1930. In the same year Frost was elected to the American Academy of Arts and Letters, and in 1931 he won a second Pulitzer Prize for his *Collected Poems* and received the Russell Loines Award for Poetry. He continued to follow a heavy lecturing schedule in order to earn extra money to support his children, who continued to suffer various health problems. Such were the demands he made on himself that his own health began to suffer, and he was unable to attend his daughter Marjorie's wedding in May 1933. Marjorie gave birth to a daughter in March 1934, but developed puerperal fever and died on 2 May within a few days of being admitted to hospital.

Further blows followed this tragedy when, in October of the same year, Elinor suffered a heart attack. For health reasons she and Frost spent the winter in Key West, Florida. During this time, as well as caring for Elinor, he was putting together his next volume of poems. In the spring of 1936 Frost was appointed Charles Eliot Norton Professor of Poetry at Harvard University, a position that involved giving a series of lectures. Later that year *A Further Range* was published, for which he was awarded his third Pulitzer Prize.

The Harvard lectures were thought by many to highlight further the growing divide in opinion on Frost and his work. Pritchard draws attention to this in *Frost: A Literary Life Reconsidered* (page 201):

> The Harvard lectures symbolized a deepening split between those
> who by this time thought of Frost as the poet for many who did
> not consider themselves connoisseurs of poetry – and those who
> (partly because of his popular reputation) condescended to him
> by allowing him limited merit, far less than what they accorded
> Eliot or Yeats or Pound.

Further tragedy was to strike the Frost family. Elinor underwent surgery for breast cancer in 1937 and the Frosts went to Florida once more to aid her recovery, but she died in 1938 after a series of heart attacks. The events of his personal life clearly took their toll on him emotionally. He resigned from Amherst College, but in 1939 he accepted a two-year appointment as Ralph Waldo Emerson Fellow in Poetry at Harvard and designated Lawrance Thompson as his 'official' biographer, stipulating that the biography must only be published after his death.

The following year Frost suffered another immense blow. His son Carol, who had been suffering for some time with severe depression, committed suicide, shooting himself with a hunting rifle on 9 October 1940. Frost travelled to his son's home to make funeral arrangements and to comfort Carol's son, who had discovered the body.

In 1941 Frost moved to Cambridge, Massachusetts, where he lived for the rest of his life, dividing his time between his house in Cambridge, the farm in Ripton, Vermont that he had brought in 1939, and Miami.

Further literary honours were to follow, and in 1943 he was awarded a fourth Pulitzer Prize for *A Witness Tree*. Frost was the first person to receive the prize four times. In 1947 *Steeple Bush* was published, and in 1949 the *Complete Poems of Robert Frost*. In 1957 he visited England again for what was to be the final time, and received honorary degrees from Durham, Oxford and Cambridge. In 1961 he was invited to take part in the inauguration of US President John F. Kennedy, and he read one of his poems at the ceremony.

Frost receives the Congressional Medal of Honor from President
Kennedy in 1962

The following year *In the Clearing* was published, and he
visited the Soviet Union at President Kennedy's request as part
of a cultural exchange programme. By now, though, his health
was failing, and on 2 December 1962 he made what was to be his
last public appearance. He died on 29 January 1963. At his final
performance, he read several of his poems and ended with *The
Road Not Taken*. It was fitting, perhaps, to choose such a popular
poem, apparently simple yet full of contradictions, to draw to a
conclusion the life of a poet in whose work simplicity so often
masks the complexities it contains.

Selected Poems of Robert Frost

Selected Poems of Robert Frost

The Pasture

I'm going out to clean the pasture spring;
I'll only stop to rake the leaves away
(And wait to watch the water clear, I may):
I shan't be gone long. – You come too.

5 *I'm going out to fetch the little calf*
That's standing by the mother. It's so young
It totters when she licks it with her tongue.
I shan't be gone long. – You come too.

from *A Boy's Will*

Ghost House

I dwell in a lonely house I know
That vanished many a summer ago,
    And left no trace but the cellar walls,
    And a cellar in which the daylight falls
5 And the purple-stemmed wild raspberries grow.

O'er ruined fences the grapevines shield
The woods come back to the mowing field;
    The orchard tree has grown one copse
    Of new wood and old where the woodpecker
    chops;
10 The footpath down to the well is healed.

I dwell with a strangely aching heart
In that vanished abode there far apart
    On that disused and forgotten road
    That has no dust-bath now for the toad.
15 Night comes; the black bats tumble and dart;

The whippoorwill is coming to shout
And hush and cluck and flutter about:
    I hear him begin far enough away
    Full many a time to say his say
20 Before he arrives to say it out.

It is under the small, dim, summer star.
I know not who these mute folk are

Who share the unlit place with me –
Those stones out under the low-limbed tree
25   Doubtless bear names that the mosses mar.

They are tireless folk, but slow and sad –
Though two, close-keeping, are lass and lad –
      With none among them that ever sings,
      And yet, in view of how many things,
30   As sweet companions as might be had.

Waiting
Afield at dusk

What things for dream there are when specter-like,
Moving among tall haycocks lightly piled,
I enter alone upon the stubble field,
From which the laborers' voices late have died,
5   And in the antiphony of afterglow
And rising full moon, sit me down
Upon the full moon's side of the first haycock
And lose myself amid so many alike.

I dream upon the opposing lights of the hour,
10 Preventing shadow until the moon prevail;
I dream upon the nighthawks peopling heaven,
Each circling each with vague unearthly cry,
Or plunging headlong with fierce twang afar;
And on the bat's mute antics, who would seem
15 Dimly to have made out my secret place,
Only to lose it when he pirouettes,
And seek it endlessly with purblind haste;
On the last swallow's sweep; and on the rasp
In the abyss of odor and rustle at my back,
20 That, silenced by my advent, finds once more,
After an interval, his instrument,
And tries once – twice – and thrice if I be there;
And on the worn book of old-golden song
I brought not here to read, it seems, but hold
25 And freshen in this air of withering sweetness;
But on the memory of one absent, most,
For whom these lines when they shall greet her eye.

Mowing

There was never a sound beside the wood but one,
And that was my long scythe whispering to the ground.
What was it it whispered? I knew not well myself;
Perhaps it was something about the heat of the sun,
5 Something, perhaps, about the lack of sound –
And that was why it whispered and did not speak.
It was no dream of the gift of idle hours,
Or easy gold at the hand of fay or elf:
Anything more than the truth would have seemed too
    weak
10 To the earnest love that laid the swale in rows,
Not without feeble-pointed spikes of flowers
(Pale orchises), and scared a bright green snake.
The fact is the sweetest dream that labor knows.
My long scythe whispered and left the hay to make.

The Tuft of Flowers

I went to turn the grass once after one
Who mowed it in the dew before the sun.

The dew was gone that made his blade so keen
Before I came to view the leveled scene.

5 I looked for him behind an isle of trees;
I listened for his whetstone on the breeze.

But he had gone his way, the grass all mown,
And I must be, as he had been – alone,

'As all must be,' I said within my heart,
10 'Whether they work together or apart.'

But as I said it, swift there passed me by
On noiseless wing a bewildered butterfly,

Seeking with memories grown dim o'er night
Some resting flower of yesterday's delight.

15 And once I marked his flight go round and round,
As where some flower lay withering on the ground.

And then he flew as far as eye could see,
And then on tremulous wing came back to me.

I thought of questions that have no reply,
20 And would have turned to toss the grass to dry;

But he turned first, and led my eye to look
At a tall tuft of flowers beside a brook,

A leaping tongue of bloom the scythe had spared
Beside a reedy brook the scythe had bared.

25 The mower in the dew had loved them thus,
By leaving them to flourish, not for us,

Nor yet to draw one thought of ours to him,
But from sheer morning gladness at the brim.

The butterfly and I had lit upon,
30 Nevertheless, a message from the dawn,

That made me hear the wakening birds around,
And hear his long scythe whispering to the ground,

And feel a spirit kindred to my own;
So that henceforth I worked no more alone;

35 But glad with him, I worked as with his aid,
And weary, sought at noon with him the shade;

And dreaming, as it were, held brotherly speech
With one whose thought I had not hoped to reach.

'Men work together,' I told him from the heart,
40 'Whether they work together or apart.'

In Hardwood Groves

The same leaves over and over again!
They fall from giving shade above,
To make one texture of faded brown
And fit the earth like a leather glove.

5 Before the leaves can mount again
To fill the trees with another shade,
They must go down past things coming up.
They must go down into the dark decayed.

They *must* be pierced by flowers and put
10 Beneath the feet of dancing flowers.
However it is in some other world
I know that this is the way in ours.

from *North of Boston*

Mending Wall

Something there is that doesn't love a wall,
That sends the frozen-ground-swell under it
And spills the upper boulders in the sun,
And makes gaps even two can pass abreast.
5 The work of hunters is another thing:
I have come after them and made repair
Where they have left not one stone on a stone,
But they would have the rabbit out of hiding,
To please the yelping dogs. The gaps I mean,
10 No one has seen them made or heard them made,
But at spring mending-time we find them there.
I let my neighbor know beyond the hill;
And on a day we meet to walk the line
And set the wall between us once again.
15 We keep the wall between us as we go.
To each the boulders that have fallen to each.
And some are loaves and some so nearly balls
We have to use a spell to make them balance:
'Stay where you are until our backs are turned!'
20 We wear our fingers rough with handling them.
Oh, just another kind of outdoor game,
One on a side. It comes to little more:
There where it is we do not need the wall:
He is all pine and I am apple orchard.
25 My apple trees will never get across
And eat the cones under his pines, I tell him.
He only says, 'Good fences make good neighbors.'
Spring is the mischief in me, and I wonder

If I could put a notion in his head:
30 '*Why* do they make good neighbors? Isn't it
Where there are cows? But here there are no cows.
Before I built a wall I'd ask to know
What I was walling in or walling out,
And to whom I was like to give offense.
35 Something there is that doesn't love a wall,
That wants it down.' I could say 'Elves' to him,
But it's not elves exactly, and I'd rather
He said it for himself. I see him there,
Bringing a stone grasped firmly by the top
40 In each hand, like an old-stone savage armed.
He moves in darkness as it seems to me,
Not of woods only and the shade of trees.
He will not go behind his father's saying,
And he likes having thought of it so well
45 He says again, 'Good fences make good neighbors.'

The Death of the Hired Man

Mary sat musing on the lamp-flame at the table,
Waiting for Warren. When she heard his step,
She ran on tiptoe down the darkened passage
To meet him in the doorway with the news
5 And put him on his guard. 'Silas is back.'
She pushed him outward with her through the door
And shut it after her. 'Be kind,' she said.
She took the market things from Warren's arms
And set them on the porch, then drew him down
10 To sit beside her on the wooden steps.

'When was I ever anything but kind to him?

But I'll not have the fellow back,' he said.
'I told him so last haying, didn't I?
If he left then, I said, that ended it.
15 What good is he? Who else will harbor him
At his age for the little he can do?
What help he is there's no depending on.
Off he goes always when I need him most.
He thinks he ought to earn a little pay,
20 Enough at least to buy tobacco with,
So he won't have to beg and be beholden.
"All right," I say, "I can't afford to pay
Any fixed wages, though I wish I could."
"Someone else can." "Then someone else will have to."
25 I shouldn't mind his bettering himself
If that was what it was. You can be certain,
When he begins like that, there's someone at him
Trying to coax him off with pocket money –
In haying time, when any help is scarce.
30 In winter he comes back to us. I'm done.'

'Sh! not so loud: he'll hear you,' Mary said.

'I want him to: he'll have to soon or late.'

'He's worn out. He's asleep beside the stove.
When I came up from Rowe's I found him here,
35 Huddled against the barn door fast asleep,
A miserable sight, and frightening, too –
You needn't smile – I didn't recognize him –
I wasn't looking for him – and he's changed.
Wait till you see.'

                    'Where did you say he'd been?'

40 'He didn't say. I dragged him to the house,
   And gave him tea and tried to make him smoke.
   I tried to make him talk about his travels.
   Nothing would do: he just kept nodding off.'

'What did he say? Did he say anything?'

45 'But little.'

            'Anything? Mary, confess
   He said he'd come to ditch the meadow for me.'

'Warren!'

        'But did he? I just want to know.'

'Of course he did. What would you have him say?
Surely you wouldn't grudge the poor old man
50 Some humble way to save his self-respect.
   He added, if you really care to know,
   He meant to clear the upper pasture, too.
   That sounds like something you have heard before?
   Warren, I wish you could have heard the way
55 He jumbled everything. I stopped to look
   Two or three times – he made me feel so queer –
   To see if he was talking in his sleep.
   He ran on Harold Wilson – you remember –
   The boy you had in haying four years since.
60 He's finished school, and teaching in his college.
   Silas declares you'll have to get him back.
   He says they two will make a team for work:
   Between them they will lay this farm as smooth!
   The way he mixed that in with other things.
65 He thinks young Wilson a likely lad, though daft

On education – you know how they fought
All through July under the blazing sun,
Silas up on the cart to build the load,
Harold along beside to pitch it on.'

70   'Yes, I took care to keep well out of earshot.'

'Well, those days trouble Silas like a dream.
You wouldn't think they would. How some things
       linger!
Harold's young college-boy's assurance piqued him.
After so many years he still keeps finding
75   Good arguments he sees he might have used.
I sympathize. I know just how it feels
To think of the right thing to say too late.
Harold's associated in his mind with Latin.
He asked me what I thought of Harold's saying
80   He studied Latin, like the violin,
Because he liked it – that an argument!
He said he couldn't make the boy believe
He could find water with a hazel prong –
Which showed how much good school had ever done
       him.
85   He wanted to go over that. But most of all
He thinks if he could have another chance
To teach him how to build a load of hay –'

'I know, that's Silas' one accomplishment.
He bundles every forkful in its place,
90   And tags and numbers it for future reference,
So he can find and easily dislodge it
In the unloading. Silas does that well.
He takes it out in bunches like big birds' nests.

You never see him standing on the hay
95 He's trying to lift, straining to lift himself.'

'He thinks if he could teach him that, he'd be
Some good perhaps to someone in the world.
He hates to see a boy the fool of books.
Poor Silas, so concerned for other folk,
100 And nothing to look backward to with pride,
And nothing to look forward to with hope,
So now and never any different.'

Part of a moon was falling down the west,
Dragging the whole sky with it to the hills.
105 Its light poured softly in her lap. She saw it
And spread her apron to it. She put out her hand
Among the harplike morning-glory strings,
Taut with the dew from garden bed to eaves,
As if she played unheard some tenderness
110 That wrought on him beside her in the night.
'Warren,' she said, 'he has come home to die:
You needn't be afraid he'll leave you this time.'

'Home,' he mocked gently.

                            'Yes, what else but home?
It all depends on what you mean by home.
115 Of course he's nothing to us, any more
Than was the hound that came a stranger to us
Out of the woods, worn out upon the trail.'

'Home is the place where, when you have to go there,
They have to take you in.'

'I should have called it
120 Something you somehow haven't to deserve.'
Warren leaned out and took a step or two,
Picked up a little stick, and brought it back
And broke it in his hand and tossed it by.
'Silas has better claim on us you think
125 Than on his brother? Thirteen little miles
As the road winds would bring him to his door.
Silas has walked that far no doubt today.

Why doesn't he go there? His brother's rich,
A somebody – director in the bank.'

130 'He never told us that.'

'We know it, though.'

'I think his brother ought to help, of course.
I'll see to that if there is need. He ought of right
To take him in, and might be willing to –
He may be better than appearances.
135 But have some pity on Silas. Do you think
If he had any pride in claiming kin
Or anything he looked for from his brother,
He'd keep so still about him all this time?'

'I wonder what's between them.'

'I can tell you.
140 Silas is what he is – we wouldn't mind him –
But just the kind that kinsfolk can't abide.
He never did a thing so very bad.
He don't know why he isn't quite as good

As anybody. Worthless though he is,
145　He won't be made ashamed to please his brother.'

'*I* can't think Si ever hurt anyone.'

'No, but he hurt my heart the way he lay
And rolled his old head on that sharp-edged
　　chair-back.
He wouldn't let me put him on the lounge.
150　You must go in and see what you can do.
I made the bed up for him there tonight.
You'll be surprised at him – how much he's broken.
His working days are done; I'm sure of it.'

'I'd not be in a hurry to say that.'

155　'I haven't been. Go, look, see for yourself.
But, Warren, please remember how it is:
He's come to help you ditch the meadow.
He has a plan. You mustn't laugh at him.
He may not speak of it, and then he may.
160　I'll sit and see if that small sailing cloud
Will hit or miss the moon.'

　　　　　　　　　　It hit the moon.
Then there were three there, making a dim row,
The moon, the little silver cloud, and she.

Warren returned – too soon, it seemed to her –
165　Slipped to her side, caught up her hand and waited.

'Warren?' she questioned.

　　　　　　　　'Dead,' was all he answered.

31

Home Burial

He saw her from the bottom of the stairs
Before she saw him. She was starting down,
Looking back over her shoulder at some fear.
She took a doubtful step and then undid it
5 To raise herself and look again. He spoke
Advancing toward her: 'What is it you see
From up there always? – for I want to know.'
She turned and sank upon her skirts at that,
And her face changed from terrified to dull.
10 He said to gain time: 'What is it you see?'
Mounting until she cowered under him.
'I will find out now – you must tell me, dear.'
She, in her place, refused him any help,
With the least stiffening of her neck and silence.
15 She let him look, sure that he wouldn't see,
Blind creature; and awhile he didn't see.
But at last he murmured, 'Oh,' and again, 'Oh.'

'What is it – what?' she said.

'Just that I see.'

'You don't,' she challenged. 'Tell me what it is.'

20 'The wonder is I didn't see at once.
I never noticed it from here before.
I must be wonted to it – that's the reason.
The little graveyard where my people are!
So small the window frames the whole of it.
25 Not so much larger than a bedroom, is it?
There are three stones of slate and one of marble,

Broad-shouldered little slabs there in the sunlight
On the sidehill. We haven't to mind *those*.
But I understand: it is not the stones,
30 But the child's mound – '

                      'Don't, don't, don't,
   don't,' she cried.

She withdrew, shrinking from beneath his arm
That rested on the banister, and slid downstairs;
And turned on him with such a daunting look,
He said twice over before he knew himself:
35 'Can't a man speak of his own child he's lost?'

'Not you – Oh, where's my hat? Oh, I don't need it!
I must get out of here. I must get air. –
I don't know rightly whether any man can.'

'Amy! Don't go to someone else this time.
40 Listen to me. I won't come down the stairs.'
He sat and fixed his chin between his fists.
'There's something I should like to ask you, dear.'

'You don't know how to ask it.'
                          'Help me, then.'

Her fingers moved the latch for all reply.

45 'My words are nearly always an offense.
I don't know how to speak of anything
So as to please you. But I might be taught,
I should suppose. I can't say I see how.
A man must partly give up being a man

50 With womenfolk. We could have some arrangement
    By which I'd bind myself to keep hands off
    Anything special you're a-mind to name.
    Though I don't like such things 'twixt those that love.
    Two that don't love can't live together without them.
55 But two that do can't live together with them.'
    She moved the latch a little. 'Don't – don't go.
    Don't carry it to someone else this time.
    Tell me about it if it's something human.
    Let me into your grief. I'm not so much
60 Unlike other folks as your standing there
    Apart would make me out. Give me my chance.
    I do think, though, you overdo it a little.
    What was it brought you up to think it the thing
    To take your mother-loss of a first child
65 So inconsolably – in the face of love.
    You'd think his memory might be satisfied –'

    'There you go sneering now!'

                        'I'm not, I'm not!
    You make me angry. I'll come down to you.
    God, what a woman! And it's come to this,
70 A man can't speak of his own child that's dead.'

    'You can't because you don't know how to speak.
    If you had any feelings, you that dug
    With your own hand – how could you? – his little grave;
    I saw you from that very window there,
75 Making the gravel leap and leap in air,
    Leap up, like that, like that, and land so lightly
    And roll back down the mound beside the hole.
    I thought, Who is that man? I didn't know you.

And I crept down the stairs and up the stairs
80 To look again, and still your spade kept lifting.
Then you came in. I heard your rumbling voice
Out in the kitchen, and I don't know why,
But I went near to see with my own eyes.
You could sit there with the stains on your shoes
85 Of the fresh earth from your own baby's grave
And talk about your everyday concerns.
You had stood the spade up against the wall
Outside there in the entry, for I saw it.'

'I shall laugh the worst laugh I ever laughed.
90 I'm cursed. God, if I don't believe I'm cursed.'

'I can repeat the very words you were saying:
"Three foggy mornings and one rainy day
Will rot the best birch fence a man can build."
Think of it, talk like that at such a time!
95 What had how long it takes a birch to rot
To do with what was in the darkened parlor?
You *couldn't* care! The nearest friends can go
With anyone to death, comes so far short
They might as well not try to go at all.
100 No, from the time when one is sick to death,
One is alone, and he dies more alone.
Friends make pretense of following to the grave,
But before one is in it, their minds are turned
And making the best of their way back to life
105 And living people, and things they understand.
But the world's evil. I won't have grief so
If I can change it. Oh, I won't, I won't!'

'There, you have said it all and you feel better.
You won't go now. You're crying. Close the door.

35

110 The heart's gone out of it: why keep it up?
      Amy! There's someone coming down the road!'

      '*You* – oh, you think the talk is all. I must go –
      Somewhere out of this house. How can I make you –'

      'If – you – do!' She was opening the door wider.
115 'Where do you mean to go? First tell me that.
      I'll follow and bring you back by force. I *will!* –'

The Black Cottage

      We chanced in passing by that afternoon
      To catch it in a sort of special picture
      Among tar-banded ancient cherry trees,
      Set well back from the road in rank lodged grass,
  5 The little cottage we were speaking of,
      A front with just a door between two windows,
      Fresh painted by the shower a velvet black.
      We paused, the minister and I, to look.
      He made as if to hold it at arm's length
 10 Or put the leaves aside that framed it in.
      'Pretty,' he said. 'Come in. No one will care.'
      The path was a vague parting in the grass
      That led us to a weathered windowsill.
      We pressed our faces to the pane. 'You see,' he said,
 15 'Everything's as she left it when she died.
      Her sons won't sell the house or the things in it.
      They say they mean to come and summer here
      Where they were boys. They haven't come this year.
      They live so far away – one is out West –
 20 It will be hard for them to keep their word.

Sand grains should sugar in the natal dew
The babe born to the desert, the sandstorm
Retard mid-waste my cowering caravans –

125 'There are bees in this wall.' He struck the clapboards
Fierce heads looked out; small bodies pivoted.
We rose to go. Sunset blazed on the windows.

After Apple-Picking

My long two-pointed ladder's sticking through a tree
Toward heaven still,
And there's a barrel that I didn't fill
Beside it, and there may be two or three
5 Apples I didn't pick upon some bough.
But I am done with apple-picking now.
Essence of winter sleep is on the night,
The scent of apples: I am drowsing off.
I cannot rub the strangeness from my sight
10 I got from looking through a pane of glass
I skimmed this morning from the drinking trough
And held against the world of hoary grass.
It melted, and I let it fall and break.
But I was well
15 Upon my way to sleep before it fell,
And I could tell
What form my dreaming was about to take.
Magnified apples appear and disappear,
Stem end and blossom end,
20 And every fleck of russet showing clear.
My instep arch not only keeps the ache,

Anyway they won't have the place disturbed.'
A buttoned haircloth lounge spread scrolling arms
Under a crayon portrait on the wall,
Done sadly from an old daguerreotype.
25 'That was the father as he went to war.
She always, when she talked about the war,
Sooner or later came and leaned, half knelt,
Against the lounge beside it, though I doubt
If such unlifelike lines kept power to stir
30 Anything in her after all the years.
He fell at Gettysburg or Fredericksburg,
I ought to know – it makes a difference which:
Fredericksburg wasn't Gettysburg, of course.
But what I'm getting to is how forsaken
35 A little cottage this has always seemed;
Since she went, more than ever, but before –
I don't mean altogether by the lives
That had gone out of it, the father first,
Then the two sons, till she was left alone.
40 (Nothing could draw her after those two sons.
She valued the considerate neglect
She had at some cost taught them after years.)
I mean by the world's having passed it by –
As we almost got by this afternoon.
45 It always seems to me a sort of mark
To measure how far fifty years have brought us.
Why not sit down if you are in no haste?
These doorsteps seldom have a visitor.
The warping boards pull out their own old nails
50 With none to tread and put them in their place.
She had her own idea of things, the old lady.
And she liked talk. She had seen Garrison
And Whittier, and had her story of them.
One wasn't long in learning that she thought,

55 Whatever else the Civil War was for,
It wasn't just to keep the States together,
Nor just to free the slaves, though it did both.
She wouldn't have believed those ends enough
To have given outright for them all she gave.
60 Her giving somehow touched the principle
That all men are created free and equal.
And to hear her quaint phrases – so removed
From the world's view today of all those things.
That's a hard mystery of Jefferson's.
65 What did he mean? Of course the easy way
Is to decide it simply isn't true.
It may not be. I heard a fellow say so.
But never mind, the Welshman got it planted
Where it will trouble us a thousand years.
70 Each age will have to reconsider it.
You couldn't tell her what the West was saying,
And what the South, to her serene belief.
She had some art of hearing and yet not
Hearing the latter wisdom of the world.
75 White was the only race she ever knew.
Black she had scarcely seen, and yellow never.
But how could they be made so very unlike
By the same hand working in the same stuff?
She had supposed the war decided that.
80 What are you going to do with such a person?
Strange how such innocence gets its own way.
I shouldn't be surprised if in this world
It were the force that would at last prevail.
Do you know but for her there was a time
85 When, to please younger members of the church,
Or rather say non-members in the church,
Whom we all have to think of nowadays,
I would have changed the Creed a very little?

Not that she ever had to ask me not to;
90 It never got so far as that; but the bare thought
Of her old tremulous bonnet in the pew,
And of her half asleep, was too much for me.
Why, I might wake her up and startle her.
It was the words "descended into Hades"
95 That seemed too pagan to our liberal youth.
You know they suffered from a general onslaught.
And well, if they weren't true why keep right on
Saying them like the heathen? We could drop them.
Only – there was the bonnet in the pew.
100 Such a phrase couldn't have meant much to her.
But suppose she had missed it from the Creed,
As a child misses the unsaid Good-night
And falls asleep with heartache – how should I feel?
I'm just as glad she made me keep hands off,
105 For, dear me, why abandon a belief
Merely because it ceases to be true.
Cling to it long enough, and not a doubt
It will turn true again, for so it goes.
Most of the change we think we see in life
110 Is due to truths being in and out of favor.
As I sit here, and oftentimes, I wish
I could be monarch of a desert land
I could devote and dedicate forever
To the truths we keep coming back and back to.
115 So desert it would have to be, so walled
By mountain ranges half in summer snow,
No one would covet it or think it worth
The pains of conquering to force change on.
Scattered oases where men dwelt, but mostly
120 Sand dunes held loosely in tamarisk
Blown over and over themselves in idleness.

It keeps the pressure of a ladder-round.
I feel the ladder sway as the boughs bend.
And I keep hearing from the cellar bin
25 The rumbling sound
Of load on load of apples coming in.
For I have had too much
Of apple-picking: I am overtired
Of the great harvest I myself desired.
30 There were ten thousand thousand fruit to touch,
Cherish in hand, lift down, and not let fall.
For all
That struck the earth,
No matter if not bruised or spiked with stubble,
35 Went surely to the cider-apple heap
As of no worth.
One can see what will trouble
This sleep of mine, whatever sleep it is.
Were he not gone,
40 The woodchuck could say whether it's like his
Long sleep, as I describe its coming on,
Or just some human sleep.

The Wood-Pile

Out walking in the frozen swamp one gray day,
I paused and said, 'I will turn back from here.
No, I will go on farther – and we shall see.'
The hard snow held me, save where now and then
5 One foot went through. The view was all in lines
Straight up and down of tall slim trees
Too much alike to mark or name a place by
So as to say for certain I was here

Or somewhere else: I was just far from home.
10 A small bird flew before me. He was careful
To put a tree between us when he lighted,
And say no word to tell me who he was
Who was so foolish as to think what *he* thought.
He thought that I was after him for a feather –
15 The white one in his tail; like one who takes
Everything said as personal to himself.
One flight out sideways would have undeceived him.
And then there was a pile of wood for which
I forgot him and let his little fear
20 Carry him off the way I might have gone,
Without so much as wishing him good-night.
He went behind it to make his last stand.
It was a cord of maple, cut and split
And piled – and measured, four by four by eight.
25 And not another like it could I see.
No runner tracks in this year's snow looped near it.
And it was older sure than this year's cutting,
Or even last year's or the year's before.
The wood was gray and the bark warping off it
30 And the pile somewhat sunken. Clematis
Had wound strings round and round it like a bundle.
What held it, though, on one side was a tree
Still growing, and on one a stake and prop,
These latter about to fall. I thought that only
35 Someone who lived in turning to fresh tasks
Could so forget his handiwork on which
He spent himself, the labor of his ax,
And leave it there far from a useful fireplace
To warm the frozen swamp as best it could
40 With the slow smokeless burning of decay.

from *Mountain Interval*

The Road Not Taken

Two roads diverged in a yellow wood,
And sorry I could not travel both
And be one traveler, long I stood
And looked down one as far as I could
5 To where it bent in the undergrowth;

Then took the other, as just as fair,
And having perhaps the better claim,
Because it was grassy and wanted wear;
Though as for that, the passing there
10 Had worn them really about the same,

And both that morning equally lay
In leaves no step had trodden black.
Oh, I kept the first for another day!
Yet knowing how way leads on to way,
15 I doubted if I should ever come back.

I shall be telling this with a sigh
Somewhere ages and ages hence:
Two roads diverged in a wood, and I –
I took the one less traveled by,
20 And that has made all the difference.

The Oven Bird

There is a singer everyone has heard,
Loud, a mid-summer and a mid-wood bird,
Who makes the solid tree trunks sound again.
He says that leaves are old and that for flowers
5 Mid-summer is to spring as one to ten.
He says the early petal-fall is past,
When pear and cherry bloom went down in showers
On sunny days a moment overcast;
And comes that other fall we name the fall.
10 He says the highway dust is over all.
The bird would cease and be as other birds
But that he knows in singing not to sing.
The question that he frames in all but words
Is what to make of a diminished thing.

Birches

When I see birches bend to left and right
Across the lines of straighter darker trees,
I like to think some boy's been swinging them.
But swinging doesn't bend them down to stay
5 As ice storms do. Often you must have seen them
Loaded with ice a sunny winter morning
After a rain. They click upon themselves
As the breeze rises, and turn many-colored
As the stir cracks and crazes their enamel.
10 Soon the sun's warmth makes them shed crystal shells
Shattering and avalanching on the snow crust –
Such heaps of broken glass to sweep away
You'd think the inner dome of heaven had fallen.

They are dragged to the withered bracken by the load,
15 And they seem not to break; though once they are bowed
So low for long, they never right themselves:
You may see their trunks arching in the woods
Years afterwards, trailing their leaves on the ground
Like girls on hands and knees that throw their hair
20 Before them over their heads to dry in the sun.
But I was going to say when Truth broke in
With all her matter of fact about the ice storm,
I should prefer to have some boy bend them
As he went out and in to fetch the cows –
25 Some boy too far from town to learn baseball,
Whose only play was what he found himself,
Summer or winter, and could play alone.
One by one he subdued his father's trees
By riding them down over and over again
30 Until he took the stiffness out of them,
And not one but hung limp, not one was left
For him to conquer. He learned all there was
To learn about not launching out too soon
And so not carrying the tree away
35 Clear to the ground. He always kept his poise
To the top branches, climbing carefully
With the same pains you use to fill a cup
Up to the brim, and even above the brim.
Then he flung outward, feet first, with a swish,
40 Kicking his way down through the air to the ground.
So was I once myself a swinger of birches.
And so I dream of going back to be.
It's when I'm weary of considerations,
And life is too much like a pathless wood
45 Where your face burns and tickles with the cobwebs
Broken across it, and one eye is weeping
From a twig's having lashed across it open.

I'd like to get away from earth awhile
And then come back to it and begin over.
50 May no fate willfully misunderstand me
And half grant what I wish and snatch me away
Not to return. Earth's the right place for love:
I don't know where it's likely to go better.
I'd like to go by climbing a birch tree,
55 And climb black branches up a snow-white trunk
Toward heaven, till the tree could bear no more,
But dipped its top and set me down again.
That would be good both going and coming back.
One could do worse than be a swinger of birches.

The Cow in Apple Time

Something inspires the only cow of late
To make no more of a wall than an open gate,
And think no more of wall-builders than fools.
Her face is flecked with pomace and she drools
5 A cider syrup. Having tasted fruit,
She scorns a pasture withering to the root.
She runs from tree to tree where lie and sweeten
The windfalls spiked with stubble and worm-eaten.
She leaves them bitten when she has to fly.
10 She bellows on a knoll against the sky.
Her udder shrivels and the milk goes dry.

An Encounter

Once on the kind of day called 'weather breeder,'
When the heat slowly hazes and the sun

By its own power seems to be undone,
I was half boring through, half climbing through
5 A swamp of cedar. Choked with oil of cedar
And scurf of plants, and weary and overheated,
And sorry I ever left the road I knew,
I paused and rested on a sort of hook
That had me by the coat as good as seated,
10 And since there was no other way to look,
Looked up toward heaven, and there against the blue,
Stood over me a resurrected tree,
A tree that had been down and raised again –
A barkless specter. He had halted too,
15 As if for fear of treading upon me.
I saw the strange position of his hands –
Up at his shoulders, dragging yellow strands
Of wire with something in it from men to men.
'You here?' I said. 'Where aren't you nowadays?
20 And what's the news you carry – if you know?
And tell me where you're off for – Montreal?
Me? I'm not off for anywhere at all.
Sometimes I wander out of beaten ways
Half looking for the orchid Calypso.'

'Out, Out –'

The buzz saw snarled and rattled in the yard
And made dust and dropped stove-length sticks of
    wood,
Sweet-scented stuff when the breeze drew across it.
And from there those that lifted eyes could count
5 Five mountain ranges one behind the other
Under the sunset far into Vermont.

47

And the saw snarled and rattled, snarled and rattled,
As it ran light, or had to bear a load.
And nothing happened: day was all but done.
10 Call it a day, I wish they might have said
To please the boy by giving him the half hour
That a boy counts so much when saved from work.
His sister stood beside them in her apron
To tell them 'Supper.' At the word, the saw,
15 As if to prove saws knew what supper meant,
Leaped out at the boy's hand, or seemed to leap –
He must have given the hand. However it was,
Neither refused the meeting. But the hand!
The boy's first outcry was a rueful laugh,
20 As he swung toward them holding up the hand,
Half in appeal, but half as if to keep
The life from spilling. Then the boy saw all –
Since he was old enough to know, big boy
Doing a man's work, though a child at heart –
25 He saw all spoiled. 'Don't let him cut my hand off –
The doctor, when he comes. Don't let him, sister!'
So. But the hand was gone already.
The doctor put him in the dark of ether.
He lay and puffed his lips out with his breath.
30 And then – the watcher at his pulse took fright.
No one believed. They listened at his heart.
Little – less – nothing! – and that ended it.
No more to build on there. And they, since they
Were not the one dead, turned to their affairs.

The Sound of Trees

I wonder about the trees.
Why do we wish to bear
Forever the noise of these
More than another noise
5 So close to our dwelling place?
We suffer them by the day
Till we lose all measure of pace,
And fixity in our joys,
And acquire a listening air.
10 They are that that talks of going
But never gets away;
And that talks no less for knowing,
As it grows wiser and older,
That now it means to stay.
15 My feet tug at the floor
And my head sways to my shoulder
Sometimes when I watch trees sway,
From the window or the door.
I shall set forth for somewhere,
20 I shall make the reckless choice
Some day when they are in voice
And tossing so as to scare
The white clouds over them on.
I shall have less to say,
25 But I shall be gone.

from *New Hampshire*

The Ax-Helve

I've known ere now an interfering branch
Of alder catch my lifted ax behind me.
But that was in the woods, to hold my hand
From striking at another alder's roots,
5 And that was, as I say, an alder branch.
This was a man, Baptiste, who stole one day
Behind me on the snow in my own yard
Where I was working at the chopping block,
And cutting nothing not cut down already.
10 He caught my ax expertly on the rise,
When all my strength put forth was in his favor,
Held it a moment where it was, to calm me,
Then took it from me – and I let him take it.
I didn't know him well enough to know
15 What it was all about. There might be something
He had in mind to say to a bad neighbor
He might prefer to say to him disarmed.
But all he had to tell me in French-English
Was what he thought of – not me, but my ax,
20 Me only as I took my ax to heart.
It was the bad ax-helve someone had sold me –
'Made on machine,' he said, plowing the grain
With a thick thumbnail to show how it ran
Across the handle's long-drawn serpentine,
25 Like the two strokes across a dollar sign.
'You give her one good crack, she's snap raght off.
Den where's your hax-ead flying t'rough de hair?'

Admitted; and yet, what was that to him?
'Come on my house and I put you one in
30 What's las' awhile – good hick'ry what's grow crooked,
De second growt' I cut myself – tough, tough!'

Something to sell? That wasn't how it sounded.

'Den when you say you come? It's cost you nothing.
Tonaght?'

As well tonight as any night.

35 Beyond an over-warmth of kitchen stove
My welcome differed from no other welcome.
Baptiste knew best why I was where I was.
So long as he would leave enough unsaid,
I shouldn't mind his being overjoyed
40 (If overjoyed he was) at having got me
Where I must judge if what he knew about an ax
That not everybody else knew was to count
For nothing in the measure of a neighbor.
Hard if, though cast away for life with Yankees,
45 A Frenchman couldn't get his human rating!

Mrs Baptiste came in and rocked a chair
That had as many motions as the world:
One back and forward, in and out of shadow,
That got her nowhere; one more gradual,
50 Sideways, that would have run her on the stove
In time, had she not realized her danger
And caught herself up bodily, chair and all,
And set herself back where she started from.
'She ain't spick too much Henglish – dat's too bad.'
55 I was afraid, in brightening first on me,

Then on Baptiste, as if she understood
What passed between us, she was only feigning.
Baptiste was anxious for her; but no more
Than for himself, so placed he couldn't hope
60 To keep his bargain of the morning with me
In time to keep me from suspecting him
Of really never having meant to keep it.

Needlessly soon he had his ax-helves out,
A quiverful to choose from, since he wished me
65 To have the best he had, or had to spare –
Not for me to ask which, when what he took
Had beauties he had to point me out at length
To insure their not being wasted on me.
He liked to have it slender as a whipstock,
70 Free from the least knot, equal to the strain
Of bending like a sword across the knee.
He showed me that the lines of a good helve
Were native to the grain before the knife
Expressed them, and its curves were no false curves
75 Put on it from without. And there its strength lay
For the hard work. He chafed its long white body
From end to end with his rough hand shut round it.
He tried it at the eyehole in the ax-head.
'Hahn, hahn,' he mused, 'don't need much taking
    down.'
80 Baptiste knew how to make a short job long
For love of it, and yet not waste time either.

Do you know, what we talked about was knowledge?
Baptiste on his defense about the children
He kept from school, or did his best to keep –
85 Whatever school and children and our doubts

Of laid-on education had to do
With the curves of his ax-helves and his having
Used these unscrupulously to bring me
To see for once the inside of his house.
90 Was I desired in friendship, partly as someone
To leave it to, whether the right to hold
Such doubts of education should depend
Upon the education of those who held them?

But now he brushed the shavings from his knee
95 And stood the ax there on its horse's hoof,
Erect, but not without its waves, as when
The snake stood up for evil in the Garden –
Top-heavy with a heaviness his short,
Thick hand made light of, steel-blue chin drawn down
100 And in a little – a French touch in that.
Baptiste drew back and squinted at it, pleased:
'See how she's cock her head!'

To E.T.

I slumbered with your poems on my breast,
Spread open as I dropped them half-read through
Like dove wings on a figure on a tomb,
To see if in a dream they brought of you

5 I might not have the chance I missed in life
Through some delay, and call you to your face
First soldier, and then poet, and then both,
Who died a soldier-poet of your race.

I meant, you meant, that nothing should remain
10 Unsaid between us, brother, and this remained –
And one thing more that was not then to say:
The Victory for what it lost and gained.

You went to meet the shell's embrace of fire
On Vimy Ridge; and when you fell that day
15 The war seemed over more for you than me,
But now for me than you – the other way.

How over, though, for even me who knew
The foe thrust back unsafe beyond the Rhine,
If I was not to speak of it to you
20 And see you pleased once more with words of mine?

Stopping by Woods on a Snowy Evening

Whose woods these are I think I know.
His house is in the village, though;
He will not see me stopping here
To watch his woods fill up with snow.

5 My little horse must think it queer
To stop without a farmhouse near
Between the woods and frozen lake
The darkest evening of the year.

He gives his harness bells a shake
10 To ask if there is some mistake.
The only other sound's the sweep
Of easy wind and downy flake.

The woods are lovely, dark, and deep,
But I have promises to keep,
15 And miles to go before I sleep,
And miles to go before I sleep.

Two Look at Two

Love and forgetting might have carried them
A little further up the mountainside
With night so near, but not much further up.
They must have halted soon in any case
5 With thoughts of the path back, how rough it was
With rock and washout, and unsafe in darkness;
When they were halted by a tumbled wall
With barbed-wire binding. They stood facing this,
Spending what onward impulse they still had
10 In one last look the way they must not go,
On up the failing path, where, if a stone
Or earthslide moved at night, it moved itself;
No footstep moved it. 'This is all,' they sighed,
'Good-night to woods.' But not so; there was more.
15 A doe from round a spruce stood looking at them
Across the wall, as near the wall as they.
She saw them in their field, they her in hers.
The difficulty of seeing what stood still,
Like some up-ended boulder split in two,
20 Was in her clouded eyes: they saw no fear there.
She seemed to think that, two thus, they were safe.
Then, as if they were something that, though strange,
She could not trouble her mind with too long,
She sighed and passed unscared along the wall.
25 '*This*, then, is all. What more is there to ask?'

But no, not yet. A snort to bid them wait.
A buck from round the spruce stood looking at them
Across the wall, as near the wall as they.
This was an antlered buck of lusty nostril,
30 Not the same doe come back into her place.
He viewed them quizzically with jerks of head,
As if to ask, 'Why don't you make some motion?
Or give some sign of life? Because you can't.
I doubt if you're as living as you look.'
35 Thus till he had them almost feeling dared
To stretch a proffering hand – and a spell-breaking.
Then he too passed unscared along the wall.
Two had seen two, whichever side you spoke from.
'This *must* be all.' It was all. Still they stood,
40 A great wave from it going over them,
As if the earth in one unlooked-for favor
Had made them certain earth returned their love.

Gathering Leaves

Spades take up leaves
No better than spoons,
And bags full of leaves
Are light as balloons.

5 I make a great noise
Of rustling all day
Like rabbit and deer
Running away.

But the mountains I raise
10 Elude my embrace,
Flowing over my arms
And into my face.

I may load and unload
Again and again
15 Till I fill the whole shed,
And what have I then?

Next to nothing for weight;
And since they grew duller
From contact with earth,
20 Next to nothing for color.

Next to nothing for use.
But a crop is a crop,
And who's to say where
The harvest shall stop?

from *West-Running Brook*

Tree at My Window

Tree at my window, window tree,
My sash is lowered when night comes on;
But let there never be curtain drawn
Between you and me.

5 Vague dream-head lifted out of the ground,
And thing next most diffuse to cloud,
Not all your light tongues talking aloud
Could be profound.

But, tree, I have seen you taken and tossed,
10 And if you have seen me when I slept,
You have seen me when I was taken and swept
And all but lost.

That day she put our heads together,
Fate had her imagination about her,
15 Your head so much concerned with outer,
Mine with inner, weather.

Acquainted with the Night

I have been one acquainted with the night.
I have walked out in rain – and back in rain.
I have outwalked the furthest city light.

I have looked down the saddest city lane.
5 I have passed by the watchman on his beat
And dropped my eyes, unwilling to explain.

I have stood still and stopped the sound of feet
When far away an interrupted cry
Came over houses from another street,

10 But not to call me back or say good-by;
And further still at an unearthly height
One luminary clock against the sky

Proclaimed the time was neither wrong nor right.
I have been one acquainted with the night.

A Soldier

He is that fallen lance that lies as hurled,
That lies unlifted now, come dew, come rust,
But still lies pointed as it plowed the dust.
If we who sight along it round the world,
5 See nothing worthy to have been its mark,
It is because like men we look too near,
Forgetting that as fitted to the sphere,
Our missiles always make too short an arc.
They fall, they rip the grass, they intersect
10 The curve of earth, and striking, break their own;
They make us cringe for metal-point on stone.
But this we know, the obstacle that checked
And tripped the body, shot the spirit on
Further than target ever showed or shone.

from A *Further Range*

Desert Places

Snow falling and night falling fast, oh, fast
In a field I looked into going past,
And the ground almost covered smooth in snow,
But a few weeds and stubble showing last.

5 The woods around it have it – it is theirs.
All animals are smothered in their lairs.
I am too absent-spirited to count;
The loneliness includes me unawares.

And lonely as it is, that loneliness
10 Will be more lonely ere it will be less –
A blanker whiteness of benighted snow
With no expression, nothing to express.

They cannot scare me with their empty spaces
Between stars – on stars where no human race is.
15 I have it in me so much nearer home
To scare myself with my own desert places.

A Leaf-Treader

I have been treading on leaves all day until I am
    autumn-tired.
God knows all the color and form of leaves I have
    trodden on and mired.
Perhaps I have put forth too much strength and been
    too fierce from fear.
I have safely trodden underfoot the leaves of another
    year.

5 All summer long they were overhead, more lifted up
    than I.
To come to their final place in earth they had to pass
    me by.
All summer long I thought I heard them threatening
    under their breath.
And when they came it seemed with a will to carry me
    with them to death.

They spoke to the fugitive in my heart as if it were leaf
    to leaf.
10 They tapped at my eyelids and touched my lips with an
    invitation to grief.
But it was no reason I had to go because they had to go.
Now up, my knee, to keep on top of another year of
    snow.

Neither Out Far nor In Deep

The people along the sand
All turn and look one way.
They turn their back on the land.
They look at the sea all day.

5 As long as it takes to pass
A ship keeps raising its hull;
The wetter ground like glass
Reflects a standing gull.

The land may vary more;
10 But wherever the truth may be –
The water comes ashore,
And the people look at the sea.

They cannot look out far.
They cannot look in deep.
15 But when was that ever a bar
To any watch they keep?

There Are Roughly Zones

We sit indoors and talk of the cold outside.
And every gust that gathers strength and heaves
Is a threat to the house. But the house has long been
    tried.
We think of the tree. If it never again has leaves,
5 We'll know, we say, that this was the night it died.
It is very far north, we admit, to have brought the
    peach.

What comes over a man, is it soul or mind –
That to no limits and bounds he can stay confined?
You would say his ambition was to extend the reach
10   Clear to the Arctic of every living kind.
Why is his nature forever so hard to teach
That though there is no fixed line between wrong and
        right,
There are roughly zones whose laws must be obeyed?
There is nothing much we can do for the tree tonight,
15   But we can't help feeling more than a little betrayed
That the northwest wind should rise to such a height
Just when the cold went down so many below.
The tree has no leaves and may never have them again.
We must wait till some months hence in the spring to
        know.
20   But if it is destined never again to grow,
It can blame this limitless trait in the hearts of men.

from A Witness Tree

The Most of It

He thought he kept the universe alone;
For all the voice in answer he could wake
Was but the mocking echo of his own
From some tree-hidden cliff across the lake.
5 Some morning from the boulder-broken beach
He would cry out on life, that what it wants
Is not its own love back in copy speech,
But counter-love, original response.
And nothing ever came of what he cried
10 Unless it was the embodiment that crashed
In the cliff's talus on the other side,
And then in the far-distant water splashed,
But after a time allowed for it to swim,
Instead of proving human when it neared
15 And someone else additional to him,
As a great buck it powerfully appeared,
Pushing the crumpled water up ahead,
And landed pouring like a waterfall,
And stumbled through the rocks with horny tread,
20 And forced the underbrush – and that was all.

A Considerable Speck
(Microscopic)

A speck that would have been beneath my sight
On any but a paper sheet so white
Set off across what I had written there.
And I had idly poised my pen in air
5　To stop it with a period of ink,
When something strange about it made me think.
This was no dust speck by my breathing blown,
But unmistakably a living mite
With inclinations it could call its own.
10　It paused as with suspicion of my pen,
And then came racing wildly on again
To where my manuscript was not yet dry;
Then paused again and either drank or smelt –
With loathing, for again it turned to fly.
15　Plainly with an intelligence I dealt.
It seemed too tiny to have room for feet,
Yet must have had a set of them complete
To express how much it didn't want to die.
It ran with terror and with cunning crept.
20　It faltered: I could see it hesitate;
Then in the middle of the open sheet
Cower down in desperation to accept
Whatever I accorded it of fate.
I have none of the tenderer-than-thou
25　Collectivistic regimenting love
With which the modern world is being swept.
But this poor microscopic item now!
Since it was nothing I knew evil of

I let it lie there till I hope it slept.
30 I have a mind myself and recognize
Mind when I meet with it in any guise.
No one can know how glad I am to find
On any sheet the least display of mind.

from *Steeple Bush*

A Young Birch

The birch begins to crack its outer sheath
Of baby green and show the white beneath,
As whosoever likes the young and slight
May well have noticed. Soon entirely white
5 To double day and cut in half the dark
It will stand forth, entirely white in bark,
And nothing but the top a leafy green –
The only native tree that dares to lean,
Relying on its beauty, to the air.
10 (Less brave perhaps than trusting are the fair.)
And someone reminiscent will recall
How once in cutting brush along the wall
He spared it from the number of the slain,
At first to be no bigger than a cane,
15 And then no bigger than a fishing pole,
But now at last so obvious a bole
The most efficient help you ever hired
Would know that it was there to be admired,
And zeal would not be thanked that cut it down
20 When you were reading books or out of town.
It was a thing of beauty and was sent
To live its life out as an ornament.

An Unstamped Letter in Our Rural Letter Box

Last night your watchdog barked all night,
So once you rose and lit the light.
It wasn't someone at your locks.
No, in your rural letter box
5 I leave this note without a stamp
To tell you it was just a tramp
Who used your pasture for a camp.
There, pointed like the pip of spades,
The young spruce made a suite of glades
10 So regular that in the dark
The place was like a city park.
There I elected to demur
Beneath a low-slung juniper
That like a blanket to my chin
15 Kept some dew out and some heat in,
Yet left me freely face to face
All night with universal space.
It may have been at two o'clock
That under me a point of rock
20 Developed in the grass and fern,
And as I woke afraid to turn
Or so much as uncross my feet,
Lest having wasted precious heat
I never should again be warmed,
25 The largest firedrop ever formed
From two stars having coalesced
Went streaking molten down the west.
And then your tramp astrologer
From seeing this undoubted stir
30 In Heaven's firm-set firmament,
Himself had the equivalent,

Only within. Inside the brain
Two memories that long had lain
Now quivered toward each other, lipped
35 Together, and together slipped;
And for a moment all was plain
That men have thought about in vain.
Please, my involuntary host,
Forgive me if I seem to boast.
40 'Tis possible you may have seen,
Albeit through a rusty screen,
The same sign Heaven showed your guest.
Each knows his own discernment best.
You have had your advantages.
45 Things must have happened to you, yes,
And have occurred to you no doubt,
If not indeed from sleeping out,
Then from the work you went about
In farming well – or pretty well.
50 And it is partly to compel
Myself, *in forma pauperis*,
To say as much I write you this.

To an Ancient

Your claims to immortality were two.
The one you made, the other one you grew.
Sorry to have no name for you but You.

We never knew exactly where to look,
5 But found one in the delta of a brook,
One in a cavern where you used to cook.

Coming on such an ancient human trace
Seems as expressive of the human race
As meeting someone living, face to face.

10 We date you by your depth in silt and dust
Your probable brute nature is discussed.
At which point we are totally nonplussed.

You made the eolith, you grew the bone,
The second more peculiarly your own,
15 And likely to have been enough alone.

You make me ask if I would go to time
Would I gain anything by using rhyme?
Or aren't the bones enough I live to lime?

The Middleness of the Road

The road at the top of the rise
Seems to come to an end
And take off into the skies.
So at the distant bend

5 It seems to go into a wood,
The place of standing still
As long the trees have stood.
But say what Fancy will,

The mineral drops that explode
10 To drive my ton of car
Are limited to the road.
They deal with near and far,

But have almost nothing to do
With the absolute flight and rest
15   The universal blue
And local green suggest.

from *In the Clearing*

A Cabin in the Clearing
For Alfred Edwards

MIST   I don't believe the sleepers in this house
Know where they are.

SMOKE   They've been here long enough
To push the woods back from around the house
And part them in the middle with a path.

5 MIST   And still I doubt if they know where they are.
And I begin to fear they never will.
All they maintain the path for is the comfort
Of visiting with the equally bewildered.
Nearer in plight their neighbors are than distance.

10 SMOKE   I am the guardian wraith of starlit smoke
That leans out this and that way from their chimney.
I will not have their happiness despaired of.

MIST   No one – not I – would give them up for lost
Simply because they don't know where they are.
15 I am the damper counterpart of smoke,
That gives off from a garden ground at night
But lifts no higher than a garden grows.
I cotton to their landscape. That's who I am.
I am no further from their fate than you are.

20 SMOKE   They must by now have learned the native
          tongue.
      Why don't they ask the Red Man where they are?

      MIST   They often do, and none the wiser for it.
      So do they also ask philosophers
      Who come to look in on them from the pulpit.
25 They will ask anyone there is to ask –
      In the fond faith accumulated fact
      Will of itself take fire and light the world up.
      Learning has been a part of their religion.

      SMOKE   If the day ever comes when they know who
30 They are, they may know better where they are.
      But who they are is too much to believe –
      Either for them or the onlooking world.
      They are too sudden to be credible.

      MIST   Listen, they murmur talking in the dark
35 On what should be their daylong theme continued.
      Putting the lamp out has not put their thought out.
      Let us pretend the dewdrops from the eaves
      Are you and I eavesdropping on their unrest –
      A mist and smoke eavesdropping on a haze –
40 And see if we can tell the bass from the soprano.

          Than smoke and mist who better could appraise
          The kindred spirit of an inner haze?

For John F. Kennedy His Inauguration

Gift outright of *The Gift Outright*
(With some preliminary history in rhyme)

Summoning artists to participate
In the august occasions of the state
Seems something artists ought to celebrate.
Today is for my cause a day of days.
5 And his be poetry's old-fashioned praise
Who was the first to think of such a thing.
This verse that in acknowledgment I bring
Goes back to the beginning of the end
Of what had been for centuries the trend;
10 A turning point in modern history.
Colonial had been the thing to be
As long as the great issue was to see
What country'd be the one to dominate
By character, by tongue, by native trait,
15 The new world Christopher Columbus found.
The French, the Spanish, and the Dutch were downed
And counted out. Heroic deeds were done.
Elizabeth the First and England won.
Now came on a new order of the ages
20 That in the Latin of our founding sages
(Is it not written on the dollar bill
We carry in our purse and pocket still?)
God nodded His approval of as good.
So much those heroes knew and understood –
25 I mean the great four, Washington,
John Adams, Jefferson, and Madison –
So much they knew as consecrated seers
They must have seen ahead what now appears:

They would bring empires down about our ears
30 And by the example of our Declaration
Make everybody want to be a nation.
And this is no aristocratic joke
At the expense of negligible folk.
We see how seriously the races swarm
35 In their attempts at sovereignty and form.
They are our wards we think to some extent
For the time being and with their consent,
To teach them how Democracy is meant.
'New order of the ages' did we say?
40 If it looks none too orderly today,
'Tis a confusion it was ours to start
So in it have to take courageous part.
No one of honest feeling would approve
A ruler who pretended not to love
45 A turbulence he had the better of.
Everyone knows the glory of the twain
Who gave America the aeroplane
To ride the whirlwind and the hurricane.
Some poor fool has been saying in his heart
50 Glory is out of date in life and art.
Our venture in revolution and outlawry
Has justified itself in freedom's story
Right down to now in glory upon glory.
Come fresh from an election like the last,
55 The greatest vote a people ever cast,
So close yet sure to be abided by,
It is no miracle our mood is high.
Courage is in the air in bracing whiffs
Better than all the stalemate an's and ifs.
60 There was the book of profile tales declaring
For the emboldened politicians daring
To break with followers when in the wrong,

A healthy independence of the throng,
A democratic form of right divine
65 To rule first answerable to high design.
There is a call to life a little sterner,
And braver for the earner, learner, yearner.
Less criticism of the field and court
And more preoccupation with the sport.
70 It makes the prophet in us all presage
The glory of a next Augustan age
Of a power leading from its strength and pride,
Of young ambition eager to be tried,
Firm in our free beliefs without dismay,
75 In any game the nations want to play.
A golden age of poetry and power
Of which this noonday's the beginning hour.

The Gift Outright

The land was ours before we were the land's.
She was our land more than a hundred years
Before we were her people. She was ours
In Massachusetts, in Virginia,
5 *But we were England's, still colonials,*
Possessing what we still were unpossessed by,
Possessed by what we now no more possessed.
Something we were withholding made us weak
Until we found out that it was ourselves
10 *We were withholding from our land of living,*
And forthwith found salvation in surrender.
Such as we were we gave ourselves outright
(The deed of gift was many deeds of war)
To the land vaguely realizing westward,
15 *But still unstoried, artless, unenhanced,*
Such as she was, such as she would become.

The Draft Horse

With a lantern that wouldn't burn
In too frail a buggy we drove
Behind too heavy a horse
Through a pitch-dark limitless grove.

5 And a man came out of the trees
And took our horse by the head
And reaching back to his ribs
Deliberately stabbed him dead.

The ponderous beast went down
10 With a crack of a broken shaft.
And the night drew through the trees
In one long invidious draft.

The most unquestioning pair
That ever accepted fate
15 And the least disposed to ascribe
Any more than we had to to hate,

We assumed that the man himself
Or someone he had to obey
Wanted us to get down
20 And walk the rest of the way.

Notes

The Pasture

Robert Frost insisted that this poem, with its relaxed, homely tone, should preface all the collected and selected editions of his poetry. Originally published in *North of Boston* and written to his wife Elinor, it can also be read as an invitation to the reader to enter the poet's chosen world: the farm with its pasture and cattle. When Eleanor Farjeon edited her selection of Frost's poetry (1960), Frost himself suggested the title, *You Come Too*.

> 2–4 **I'll only stop... be gone long**   Note the references to time here – a major theme in Frost's poetry.

from *A Boy's Will*
Ghost House

This poem achieves its impact by striking the same note of unresolved mystery as Walter de la Mare's *The Listeners* and Rudyard Kipling's *The Way Through the Woods*. How can the speaker be dwelling in a lonely house which *vanished many a summer ago* (2)? Why is the speaker's heart *strangely aching* (11), and what is he referring to when he says *in view of how many things* (29)? Above all, who or what is the speaker – is he himself a ghost?

> 16 **whippoorwill**   nightjar.
> 25 **mar**   spoil; the moss covers over the names on the gravestones under the tree.
> 26 **They are tireless folk**   This is another puzzle – how does the speaker know things about the couple but yet not know who they are?
> 27 **close-keeping**   keeping close to each other, or keeping themselves to themselves.

Waiting

The importance of dreams and dreaming as a way of approaching reality is a theme not only in this poem but also in *Mowing* (page 21) and *After Apple-Picking* (page 40). What does the subtitle, *Afield at dusk*, add to your understanding of the poem? Notice the roundabout way in which this poem arrives at its conclusion – how and why do the last two lines make you re-read the whole of the rest of the poem?

2   **haycocks**   haystacks.

4   **late**   recently.

5   **antiphony**   literally, singing or chanting by two alternating choirs; here the last light of sunset on the one hand and the first light of the full moon rising on the other.

9   **the opposing lights**   i.e. the sunset and the rising moon referred to in the previous stanza.

16   **pirouettes**   turns circles, like a dancer.

17   **purblind**   unable to see clearly.

18–19   **rasp/In the abyss of odor**   a grating sound made by an animal (a fieldmouse?). Because it is dusk, the field has become indistinct – the speaker is aware only of the great space (*the abyss*) and the strong smell of the cut hay.

20   **advent**   coming.

23   **the worn book of old-golden song**   The book is presumably worn because it has been well-used, and has been well-used because it contains much-loved and familiar songs from the past. What is this image intended to convey at this point in the poem?

27   The person for whom this poem is intended as a gift once she reads it.

Mowing

This sonnet centres on the paradoxes expressed in lines 9 and 13: *Anything more than the truth would have seemed too weak* and *The fact is the sweetest dream that labor knows*. These paradoxes are central to Frost's poetry, and go a long way towards providing a key to his writing. His poems are often notable for a seemingly dogged determination to present the facts and details of a situation, no matter how trivial. By this means, rather than through generalization, Frost achieves an unusual degree of realism and challenges the reader to deny the *truth* (9) of what is being described. (For a discussion of Frost's treatment of nature see Interpretations, page 112.)

Mowing is the poem which Frost himself thought the most successful in his first volume, *A Boy's Will*. How do you think it compares with the other poems from his first book, selected here?

8 **fay**   fairy, spirit.
10 **swale**   low-lying piece of ground.
12 **orchises**   orchids.

The Tuft of Flowers

In this poem the speaker moves from a belief that everyone lives essentially alone (lines 8–10) to a conviction that '*Men work together... Whether they work together or apart*' (39–40). How does he come to change his view so completely?

Frost's expression of delight in this poem at the work of the mower and what he learns from him can be compared with Wordsworth's poems *The Leech Gatherer* and *The Solitary Reaper*. Both of these poems pay tribute to the essential dignity and wisdom of those who undertake solitary manual work and thus achieve a close understanding of, and sympathy with, nature.

6 **whetstone**   a stone on which the mower would sharpen the blade of his scythe.
12 **a bewildered butterfly**   In what sense is the butterfly bewildered, and what significance does he have for the speaker?
23 **A leaping tongue of bloom**   This is like a tongue of flame – perhaps an echo of the biblical story of the tongues of flame representing the Holy Spirit which descended on the Apostles at Pentecost (Acts 2:3). For the speaker (and for the butterfly) the tuft of flowers offers an epiphany, a moment of revelation and inspiration – *a message from the*

dawn (30) – which brings him into closer harmony with nature.

33 **a spirit kindred to my own**   The speaker feels such an affinity with the mower (even though he cannot see him) that from now on it is as if they are working in the field together.

In Hardwood Groves

This poem illustrates again Frost's ability to present simple but essential truths on the basis of his observation of nature. The symbolism suggests the theme of death and resurrection that appears elsewhere in Frost's poetry. Lines 7 and 8 suggest a childlike intuition of things as they really are. What is the impact and significance of the triple repetition of *must* (7–9)?

Title **Hardwood**   i.e. deciduous trees which lose their leaves in autumn.

11 **However it is**   whatever the situation may be. The speaker observes the cycle of death and re-birth (leaves falling, being turned to compost; shoots of new plants forcing their way up through the dead leaves). It is essential, the poem implies, to accept things simply as they are.

from *North of Boston*
Mending Wall

This is one of Frost's most anthologized poems but ironically many readers have mistakenly assumed that Frost's own philosophy of human relationships can be summed up in the statement '*Good fences make good neighbors*' (45) because the poem ends with this line. In fact, the poem proclaims Frost's belief that walls (and barriers of any kind) *give offense* (34). Yet is his attitude as unambiguous as he implies? After all, it is the speaker who has agreed to assist his neighbour in mending the wall, rather than let it collapse altogether; indeed, he initiates the process. Perhaps the poem's power lies in the tension between the neighbour's conviction that barriers are a good thing and the narrator's more tentative position – *Something there is that doesn't love a wall* (1). What is achieved by calling the poem *Mending Wall* rather than 'Mending a Wall'?

The distinctive form of the poem (unrhyming, decasyllabic – ten-syllable – lines) and the colloquial style of the monologue enable Frost to create a style and tone of voice which he will use frequently in later narrative poems (e.g. *The Death of the Hired Man*, page 25 and *Home Burial*, page 32). Inversions such as the opening line (*Something there is...*) and his use of amplification to make clearer what he wants to say (e.g. *The gaps I mean,/No one has seen them made* [9–10]) all become characteristic features of Frost's style.

5 **another thing**   a different case.

24 *Pine* and *apple orchard* are the two types of woodland on either side of the wall.

28 **Spring is the mischief in me**   spring makes me feel mischievous. Note that the speaker only wonders *If I could put a notion in his head* (29). The things he would like to say to his neighbour remain unsaid, so the rest of the poem becomes, in effect, an argument that the speaker has with himself.

40 **an old-stone savage**   a primitive stone-age hunter. (Compare with *To an Ancient*, page 69.) Is the speaker making an ironic comment on his neighbour's primitive views of social relationships – hence line 41?

41 **He moves in darkness**   The speaker feels that his neighbour has never developed his own philosophy of life; instead *He will not go behind his father's saying* (43). By contrast the speaker prefers to see barriers between people coming down, not going up: see lines 32–4.

The Death of the Hired Man

This poem forms a striking contrast with *Home Burial* (page 32). Far from the sense of failure and breakdown in communication evident in the latter poem, *The Death of the*

Hired Man centres on a relationship and on a home built on trust and affection. Nevertheless, even here there are tensions and disagreements between the husband and the wife. The central section of the poem (lines 11–120) consists of a dialogue between Mary and Warren, a young couple running a farm, in which they discuss whether it would be appropriate to allow an old and by now incompetent farm hand to have his job back. Frost himself had had experience both of working as a hired man (a casual farm labourer) and of running his own farm. (See pages 2–5.)

30 **I'm done**   I can't take any more.

58 **He ran on Harold Wilson**   The hired man keeps talking about one of his former workmates.

63 **lay this farm**   cut all the hay in the fields belonging to the farm.

73 **piqued**   irritated, got under his skin.

83 He knew how to locate underground springs by water-divining (dowsing) with a forked branch of hazel held in the hands.

98 **the fool of books**   Silas believes that the boy (Harold Wilson) will look a fool if he spends his time reading rather than learning practical skills.

107 **the harplike morning-glory strings**   Morning glory is a climbing plant (often wild). Its tendrils here stretch right from the ground to the eaves of the house.

118 **Home is the place**   The two definitions of home offered here and in lines 119–120 emphasize the value placed on home by Mary and Warren. The importance of home for them makes Silas's homelessness all the more poignant – hence the significance of Mary's comment *he has come home to die* (111).

134 **better than appearances**   more kindhearted than his behaviour so far has suggested.

141 **kinsfolk**   relatives, members of the same family.

160–3 It is characteristic of Frost that he focuses our attention (and Mary's) on an apparently trivial detail – whether or not a small cloud covers the moon as it sails past – while a momentous event (the death of the hired man) is being discovered by her husband.

162 **making a dim row**   the moon, the cloud and Mary; they are only dimly seen because the cloud drifts across the moon.

Home Burial

On one level, this is one of the most clearly autobiographical of Frost's poems. His own son, Elliott, died in infancy in 1900, putting a severe strain on his relationship with his wife, Elinor. Frost's biographer, Lawrance Thompson (*Robert Frost: A Biography*, page 116) speaks of the 'unhealed wound of his grief over Elliott's death' and comments that 'Inseparable from that grief was his puzzled awareness that his relationship with Elinor had not developed as he had hoped.' *Home Burial* is not simply autobiographical, however. From its opening words: *He saw her from the bottom of the stairs* (1), it presents an impersonal account of a failing relationship which is at once private and universal. The title refers not only to the child buried within sight of the house where its parents live but also to the sense in which both the man and the woman have been buried alive in a house and in a marriage from which they cannot escape. Their relationship has become a kind of living death. As in *Mending Wall* (page 24) the barriers created by the walls of the house are psychological more than physical.

12 **you must tell me, dear**   The term *dear* seems so inadequate here (and again in line 42), as if to imply a failure of true feeling. The man is aware that his wife is troubled (as line 3, describing her behaviour on the stairs – *Looking back over her shoulder at some fear* – implies) but is unable to find the right words or tone to reach her.

49–50 **A man must partly give up being a man/With womenfolk**   What do these lines suggest about the man's experience of marriage? Do they affect your attitude towards him?

59–62 The husband's failure to understand the woman's grief and anger is expressed in the limp assurance that he is *not so much/Unlike other folks* (59–60) and his comment *I do think, though, you overdo it a little* (62).

89–90 The husband speaks here. Do you think that he seriously believes he is cursed, or is he trying to use sarcasm to make light of his wife's criticism of his apparent lack of feeling over the death of their child?

102–5 The woman's complaint about people's inability to face death and to sustain grief is the poem's central point. By saying *before one is in it* (103), the wife seems almost to imply her own death. On the other hand, these lines can be taken to imply the poet's attitude – that one has to accept and endure life. (Compare with '*Out, Out –*', page 47 where a similar theme is explored.)

116 What does the poem's abrupt and inconclusive ending suggest about the man's final understanding of his wife's feelings? Why does Frost frequently end his poems on an unresolved note like this?

The Black Cottage

The central idea of this poem is summed up in the paradoxical remark:

'For, dear me, why abandon a belief
Merely because it ceases to be true.'   (105–6)

Significantly, Frost turns a question into a statement by refusing to use a question mark. *The Black Cottage* is an important example of a narrative poem in which nothing actually happens, but a chance encounter or observation sets off a chain of thought or memory which becomes the poetic focus of Frost's imagination. From a negative opening (the abandoned cottage passed by chance) the poem moves slowly towards the conclusion that beliefs don't become invalid just because they go out of fashion:

'Most of the change we think we see in life
Is due to truths being in and out of favor.'   (109–10)

(For a further discussion of this poem, see Interpretations page 136.)

3 **tar-banded**   Tar is often used as part of the process of grafting fruit trees.
22 **A buttoned haircloth lounge**   an upholstered settee or sofa.
24 **daguerreotype**   an early form of photograph.
25 **war**   the American Civil War.
31 **Gettysburg or Fredericksburg**   battles in the American Civil War, in 1863 and 1862 respectively.
41 **the considerate neglect**   The old woman had taught her sons to be independent and did not mind that they rarely came back to visit her.
52–3 **Garrison/And Whittier**   William Lloyd Garrison (1805–79) and John

Greenleaf Whittier (1807–92) were leading figures in the movement to abolish slavery. Whittier was one of the most celebrated American poets of the nineteenth century, best remembered today for his hymn 'Dear Lord and Father of Mankind'.

61   This is a principle enshrined in the opening statement of the American Declaration of Independence (1776):

We hold these truths to be self-evident, that all men are created equal and that they are endowed by their Creator with certain unalienable Rights, that among these are Life, Liberty and the pursuit of Happiness.

64   **Jefferson's**   Thomas Jefferson, third American President and principal author of the Declaration of Independence.

68   **the Welshman**   Jefferson claimed Welsh ancestry.

74   **latter**   more recent.

88   **Creed**   the statement of Christian faith, beginning: *I believe...*

94   **"descended into Hades"**   In the Creed, it is stated that Jesus *descended into hell*. In classical Greek mythology, Hades was the underworld.

119–24   The minister gives a detailed description of the *desert land* he would like to be *monarch* of: it would have *Scattered oases* (119), *Sand dunes* (120), and a child born in the desert there would find its body covered with grains of sand like a sprinkling of sugar. It would not be a hospitable land because the unfashionable *truths we keep coming back and back to* (114) are not the truths that are popular.

120   **tamarisk**   a shrub found on seashores.

125   **clapboards**   weatherboarding on the outside of the cottage.

After Apple-Picking

This poem, with its free verse-form and its relaxed, present-tense, first-person description, takes Frost into a new direction which will be increasingly important in his poetry. Out of an intensely experienced and documented moment – looking out on the scene where the apple-picking has been happening – the poet is able to confront truths about himself and to ask questions about what lies beyond human experience. It is worth comparing this poem with Keats's *Ode to a Nightingale* to see how both writers present the idea of sleep and death. Note also the set of contrasts on which the poem is built: summer/winter, work/rest, effort/reward, sleep/wakefulness; how do these contrasts contribute to the poem's effect?

7 **Essence of winter sleep**   The scent of the apples reminds the speaker of hibernation. Apples used to be stored in darkened rooms to preserve them for eating throughout the winter. These apple-stores had a very distinctive smell, rather like home-made dry cider.

10 **glass**   ice.

22 **ladder-round**   the rung on which he has been standing.

40 **woodchuck**   a North American marmot, a squirrel-like rodent, also known as a groundhog.

41 **Long sleep**   hibernation (an echo of line 7).

The Wood-Pile

Like *After Apple-Picking* (page 40), this poem is a meditation sparked by a seemingly trivial but vivid moment of experience. The pile of wood prompts the speaker to ask who could take such trouble over a task and then apparently forget about it (see lines 34–7).

This poem has a bleakness emphasized at the start by Frost defining the place and the time of his experience as *the frozen swamp one gray day* (1) and culminating in the final image of the *slow smokeless burning of decay* (40).

23 **a cord of maple**   A cord is a measure of cut wood, usually 128 cubic feet. The maple tree is found everywhere in North America and Canada (the maple leaf is the Canadian flag's emblem).

30 **Clematis**   a climbing plant. During spring and summer clematis has a profusion of flowers, but in winter only its rope-like tendrils can be seen.

from *Mountain Interval*
The Road Not Taken

This poem, which Robert Frost claimed was about his friend, the poet Edward Thomas (see Interpretations page 130), is one of his best-known but most problematic poems. The title suggests that the subject is the road, the choice that the speaker did not take; the reader is apparently invited to ask whether the speaker regrets not having taken that road, or at least whether he regrets not having had the chance to explore both the roads that *diverged in a yellow wood* (1). However, the poem actually focuses on the road that *was* chosen, and the last line leaves open the question: exactly what is the *difference* (20) which choosing the less-travelled road has made? Thus, although the poem appears to be a brave assertion of the value of making unconventional decisions in life, it may also be read as a world-weary acknowledgement that you have to go on living with the consequences of your choices:

> I shall be telling this with a sigh
> Somewhere ages and ages hence: (16–17)

William H. Pritchard (*Frost: A Literary Life Reconsidered*, page 128) describes *The Road Not Taken* as 'a notable instance in Frost's work of a poem which sounds noble but is really mischievous.' Ian Hamilton says:

> The air of lostness, of irretrievable error that hangs over the poem is a beguiling means of disguising its essentially inert bleakness. To Frost, it doesn't seem to matter much which road he took, or didn't take. It is that indifference which should have been the real subject of the poem. (*Robert Frost: Selected Poems*, pages 18–19)

The poem's unusually taut verse-form (nine-syllable lines, rhyming *abaab*) contrasts with its apparently casual tone (*perhaps the better claim* [7], *really about the same* [10], *I doubted if I should ever come back* [15]).

1 **yellow wood**   i.e. in autumn. The paths are covered in fallen leaves (see line 12). Does this imply a choice made late on in life? (This would be appropriate if the poem is about Edward Thomas: Thomas had to choose in his late thirties whether to join up and fight in the First World War or whether to follow Frost's suggestion and emigrate to America.)

8 **wanted wear**   lacked use; no one had walked this way lately so the grass had not been trodden down.

16 By using the future tense in this line, the speaker implies that his journey has not yet come to an end.

The Oven Bird

This poem, in the form of a rather unconventional sonnet, illustrates Frost's particular strain of pessimism. At the height of midsummer, the speaker is already anticipating autumn, *that other fall we name the fall* (9). The bird who sings is (according to Jeffrey Meyers, *Robert Frost: A Biography*, page 138) 'an American warbler with an oven-shaped nest' and the question with which the poem ends (*what to make of a diminished thing* [14]) invites the reader to accept that life itself, like the summer, is past its best. Alternatively, the question could be seen as a challenge: just as the bird – although he senses the onset of autumn – is able to fill the wood with his singing, how can we celebrate a life which is less than perfect? Frost explores the bird's ability to celebrate life as a temporary phenomenon and thereby to transcend it.

12 **he knows in singing not to sing**   Although the bird sounds cheerful he knows that the future is nothing to sing about.

14 **a diminished thing**   something that is no longer as fine or impressive or desirable as it used to be.

Birches

Drawing on his own childhood memories, Frost creates an image (birch trees bent almost to the ground by a child who climbs and swings on them) that sums up all the ambiguity which as an adult he feels about life:

> I'd like to get away from earth awhile
> And then come back to it and begin over. (48–9)

Look carefully at the last six lines of the poem: what meaning and feeling can you discern behind the line *One could do worse than be a swinger of birches* (59)? Robert Frost wrote that '*Birches* is two fragments soldered together so long I have forgotten where the join is.' Can you locate it?

5 **Often you must have seen them** Notice how the speaker draws the reader into the poem. This single reference to *you* turns the poem from a private meditation into a monologue directed at a listener. This idea is reinforced in line 21: *But I was going to say when Truth broke in.*

44 **life is too much like a pathless wood** This image (is it a cliché?) is one that was shared both by Frost and by Edward Thomas.

56 *Toward* Why does Frost put this word in italics?

The Cow in Apple Time

In this poem the poet seems to be amused by the drunken cow but characteristically the last line strikes a very different note: the cow is no longer an image of fun but of scorn and decay. How does the unusual rhyme scheme of this poem enhance and emphasize the poet's point of view?

3 **wall-builders** See *Mending Wall* (page 24).

4 **pomace** the pulp of apples after they have been crushed for cider making.

8 **windfalls** apples that have been blown off the tree or have fallen of their own accord. (See *After Apple-Picking*, page 40.)

10 **knoll** small hill.

11 Look carefully at this last line; why does the poem end with these images of uselessness?

An Encounter

Out of an almost comical insight – that a telegraph pole is both *a resurrected tree* (12) and *A barkless specter* (14) – and an equally comical encounter (the speaker talks to the telegraph pole about the destination of the messages being carried along its wires), Frost creates a poem in which the speaker acknowledges his own apparent lack of direction (though not entirely his lack of purpose):

> 'Me? I'm not off for anywhere at all.
> Sometimes I wander out of beaten ways
> Half looking for the orchid Calypso.'   (22–4)

What is the effect of the intricate irregular rhyme-scheme of this poem?

1 **'weather breeder'**   Perhaps this is the sort of atmosphere that seems to be building up to a thunder storm and a change in the weather.

6–7 **and weary and overheated,/And sorry**   The repetition of *and* emphasizes the speaker's sense of discomfort and annoyance with himself.

7 **sorry I ever left the road I knew**   See *The Road Not Taken* (page 43).

12 **a resurrected tree**   This image, amplified by the next line (*A tree that had been down and raised again*) deliberately borrows the language of Christianity in echoing the idea of Christ's death and resurrection.

24 **Calypso**   in Greek mythology, the queen of an island (probably Gozo, near Malta) where Ulysses was shipwrecked. She kept him there for seven years, promising him perpetual youth if he remained faithful to her. Calypso is also the name of a rare orchid found in North America, also called Lady's Slipper or Moccasin.

'Out, Out –'

The impact of this poem springs from two shocks: first, the loss of the hand in the accident with the saw, and then the death of the boy. These events seem the more shocking because of the impersonal tone of the narrative (*So. But the hand was gone already* [27]) and the apparent indifference to tragedy reflected in the final sentence: *And they, since they/Were not the one dead, turned to their affairs* (33–4). Note the use of half-rhyme in this poem – with its lack of resolution. What does it contribute to the impact of the writing?

Title **'Out, Out –'**   See *Macbeth*: 'Out, out brief candle!' A line from the soliloquy, spoken by Macbeth, after he has been told of the death of his wife. He speaks of the apparent pointlessness and brevity of life.

12   **when saved from work**   Ironically the half-hour of free time would have saved his life.

23–4   **big boy/Doing a man's work, though a child at heart**   How well does this reflect Frost's ambiguous feelings about himself and his life?

28   **the dark of ether**   the anaesthetic, but also anticipating the darkness of death.

33–4   Compare the apparent indifference of the adults here with the complaints of the wife in *Home Burial* (page 32) of the callous attitude of people towards the death of her child. What does the reaction of the adults to the child's death in this poem tell us about these people and their lifestyle?

The Sound of Trees

By contrast with Frost's more usual decasyllabic (ten-syllable) lines, the short lines of *The Sound of Trees* give the poem an unsettling tone which is reflected in the speaker's certainty that one day he will *make the reckless choice* (20) even though he does not yet know where that choice will lead him. Some of the deliberately awkward phrases (e.g. *They are that that talks of going* [10], and *tossing so as to scare/The white clouds over them on* [22–23]) help to reinforce the sense of dislocation. Why does the speaker include a second person in lines 2–5 (*Why do we wish to bear... our dwelling place?*) when, by line 16, he is speaking as if he is an isolated figure (*my head sways... I shall set forth for somewhere*)? The poem seems to end with the speaker's final, almost unnoticed, disappearance:

> I shall have less to say,
> But I shall be gone. (24–5)

> 3 **the noise of these** Is it just the trees that will drive the narrator away with their incessant noise or are they a metaphor for something else? Words such as *bear* (2), *suffer* (6) and *scare* (22) all suggest a pain that has a human source.

from *New Hampshire*
The Ax-Helve

Although the title suggests that this poem has as its central theme or image the handle (helve) of an axe, Frost presents several topics here: in particular, he is concerned with the way people (in this instance, neighbours) create relationships while at the same time maintaining a sense of distance. (Compare with *Mending Wall*, page 24.) The poem also focuses on the question of education and what rights being educated confers on people. It is as if the speaker himself is surprised to find such a topic emerging in the conversation he has when he visits his neighbour: *Do you know, what we talked about was knowledge?* (82).

The Ax-Helve is a rare example of Frost's use of dialect in a poem – in this case the French-English idiom of the neighbour Baptiste: the awkwardness of his speech (*She ain't spick too much Henglish – dat's too bad* [54]) reflects his own awkward but persistent personality. (See Interpretations page 145.)

> 2 **alder** a tree of the same variety as the birch, with catkins and serrated leaves.

5 **as I say**   Note the relaxed tone achieved here by the use of near repetition so early in the poem.

24 **the handle's long-drawn serpentine**   the distinctive curving shape of the axe handle.

30 **good hick'ry**   Hickory is a tough, heavy wood from which walking sticks and tool-handles are often made.

38–43 This very complex sentence (itself almost serpentine like the handle of the axe) reflects the difficulty the two men have in weighing each other up. The speaker isn't going to let himself be worried by the position in which he has been placed. He will have to judge whether Baptiste's expert knowledge about axes gives him a special claim to be respected as a neighbour.

44 **Yankees**   slang term for the inhabitants of New England or one of the northern United States. Frost himself came from this area.

69 **whipstock**   the handle of a whip.

76 **chafed**   rubbed.

78 **the eyehole in the ax-head**   the hole into which the handle of the axe is fitted.

83 **on his defense**   on the defensive.

90–3 Another 'serpentine' sentence. As in lines 38–43 above, here the speaker has to make up his mind about what Baptiste wants from him as a neighbour: 'Did Baptiste want me as a friend partly because he could trust me to decide whether he was well enough educated to be entitled to have his own views on how his children should be educated?'

97 This is a reference to the serpent that tempts Eve to eat the apple from the tree of the knowledge of good and evil, as described in the Bible (Genesis 3:1–16). The serpent was often depicted (e.g. in stained glass windows) as standing erect or twining around the trunk of the tree – hence it *stood up for evil* (97).

To E. T.

Robert Frost's friendship with Edward Thomas was one of the most significant of his life. (See pages 7–9.) Thomas was killed in action during the Battle of Arras in April 1917.

This poem, addressed to Thomas himself, is strikingly formal (by Frost's standards) in its structure and diction: calling Thomas *a soldier-poet of your race* (8) is a most un-Frost like phrase. As in *The Road Not Taken* (p.28) Frost meditates here on choices and opportunities missed. Here too Frost is not afraid to couch difficult ideas in complex and obscure statements. Lines 9–12, the central stanza of the poem, seem to defy interpretation. What Frost means by *The Victory for what it lost and gained* (12) is obscured by the syntax of the sentence in which it appears. By contrast, the poem ends with a touchingly simple final question which is intended to reflect the delight that Frost took in Thomas's friendship and in their shared experience of poetry.

Why do you think Frost identifies Thomas only by his initials in the title of this poem?

3 Interestingly, Frost presents himself here as an effigy, a carved stone figure on top of a tomb, covered by the wings of doves, the symbol of peace.

13 Thomas was killed by a shell during the Battle of Arras (*Vimy Ridge* [14]).

18 **beyond the Rhine**   i.e. into Germany. There was continuing anxiety in Europe and America during the 1920s and 1930s that Germany (*The foe* – note again the formal, poetic language) would provoke another war.

Stopping by Woods on a Snowy Evening

Along with *The Road Not Taken* (page 43) this is one of the best known of Frost's poems. It is also one of the most troubling, and some critics have suggested that its underlying theme is suicide. The title seems to suggest the caption for a picture or photograph, as if the poem is a snapshot in words. And yet Frost is not simply concerned to paint a scene, for behind the images (woods, snow, midwinter – *The darkest evening of the year* [8]) and the almost child-like rhythms and rhyme scheme lies the idea of a choice that is dangerously tempting. In the final stanza *The woods are lovely, dark, and deep* (13) but the speaker is held back from entering them by the promises, the commitments, which will force him to continue his journey. He may literally have *miles to go* (15) before he can rest, but the repetition of the line may also suggest that he realizes he has to live out the rest of his life before he can die (*sleep* [15–16]).

2 **His**   As with *Whose* in line 1, the speaker does not identify the owner of the woods. At the outset, therefore, a note of mystery and anxiety is created.

5 **My little horse**   What use is made of the horse and of the owner of the woods in the poem?

8 It is the winter solstice (21 December). Compare with John Donne's poem A *Nocturnal upon St Lucie's Day*, which is set on the same day.

13 Some manuscript versions of the text of this poem omit the comma after the word *dark*. What difference would this make to a reading of the line and, perhaps, of the poem as a whole?

Two Look at Two

This poem is set in Frost's familiar landscape: woods, paths, and walls all feature not as background but as setting for an encounter between a human couple and a doe and a buck. The meeting forces the man and woman to reassess and perhaps to reaffirm the importance of their relationship. The querulous tone in which, the poet suggests, the buck addresses the human couple: '*Why don't you make some motion?/Or give some sign of life? Because you can't.*'(32–3) is reminiscent of the anguished wife in *Home Burial* (page 32). The ending of the poem (lines 39–42) suggests a kind of epiphany (a moment of insight or intuition) in which the true nature of their relationship (and of humanity's relationship with nature) is revealed to the man and woman.

6 **washout**   This is a geological technical term. Frost is referring to a narrow river channel that cuts into pre-existing sediment. Here, the path is partially washed away.

27 **A buck from round the spruce**   Compare with *The Most of It* (page 64), lines 10–20, where another buck makes a dramatic appearance.

Gathering Leaves

Frost's use of a very compact verse-form means that the lines of this poem are presented as a series of aphorisms (statements of general truths). The physical description of gathering leaves (stanzas 1–3) leads on in stanza 4 to a universal question about how to put a value on work that has been done.

10 **Elude**   avoid, escape.

from *West-Running Brook*
Tree at My Window

In poems such as *Birches* (p.30) and *The Sound of Trees* (p.35) Frost has produced meditations prompted by trees; in this poem the speaker addresses a tree directly. The writing is notable for its strikingly original description of the tree (*Vague dream-head lifted out of the ground,/And thing next most diffuse to cloud*, [5–6]) and for the sense of shared identity that the speaker feels. The poem is also distinguished for its careful modulation (deliberate variation) of tone: look particularly at the effect achieved by the use of the short fourth line of each stanza.

2 **sash**   the lower portion of the window.
7 **your light tongues talking aloud**   the leaves rustling in the wind.
13 Compare the way the speaker here manages to identify with the tree (while carefully insisting on the difference between them) with the way the speaker compares and contrasts himself with the leaves in A *Leaf-Treader* (page 61). Note also the wit of the analogy.

Acquainted with the Night

The use of repetition in this poem, both of whole lines and of phrases, helps to establish an almost chant-like effect, which is emphasized by the inter-linking rhyme scheme. (See *Preludes* and *The Love Song of J. Alfred Prufrock* by T.S. Eliot and *As I Walked Out One Evening* by W.H. Auden for other contemporary poems where the speaker has been 'acquainted with the night' and the setting is a bleak urban night landscape.) How does Frost establish the tone of this poem, and what clues does the tone offer about the reasons for the speaker's solitary walking?

    12 **luminary**   not just lit up, but light-giving.

A Soldier

Written in the form of a sonnet, this poem (rather like *To E.T.*, page 53) adopts a formal, impersonal note. How does his use of diction enable Frost to achieve this note? From the opening line with its description of the soldier as *that fallen lance* (an example of synecdoche, where the whole being – the soldier – is represented by one of his parts – his fallen lance) onwards, Frost develops the idea of the soldier and his sacrifice as somehow greater than ordinary human endeavours: *Our missiles always make too short an arc* (8).

     7 **as fitted to the sphere**   The *sphere* here refers to earth; as men and women we take too limited (earth-bound) a view of life and its potential.

12–14 Frost ends the poem with the assertion (*But this we know* [12]) that at the moment of death, the soldier's soul escapes the limits of the body and of this world. This is one of the rare occasions in Frost's poetry where the idea of an afterlife is clearly implied.

from A *Further Range*
Desert Places

This poem should be compared with *Stopping by Woods on a Snowy Evening* (p.41) and with *Tree at My Window* (p.45). The sense of physical and emotional isolation (*I am too absent-spirited to count* [7]) is strongly emphasized by the image of the falling snow (*A blanker whiteness* [11]). However, the speaker is not frightened by isolated places but by his sense of spiritual emptiness. The final stanza's insistence on the *empty spaces* (13) magnifies the speaker's fear of his own inner loneliness:

> I have it in me so much nearer home
> To scare myself with my own desert places. (15–16)

Thus the natural scene becomes a symbol of a state of mind – a common use of symbolism in Frost's poetry.

5 The first *it* refers to the *field* (2); the repeated *it – it* emphasizes how the snow is becoming part of the landscape.

8 **includes** envelopes or embraces.

11 **benighted** literally, overtaken by darkness; metaphorically, morally and spiritually empty.

16 **scare** Note the choice of a colloquial term here. What does it contribute to the poem that an alternative word such as 'terrify' might not have done?

A Leaf-Treader

Leaves are an important recurring image in Frost's poetry. (See Interpretations page 115.) Compare this poem with *Gathering Leaves* (page 56); in what ways are the final stanzas of each poem similar to, and different from, each other?

2 **mired** covered in mud.

4 **the leaves of another year** Having trodden down the leaves into the compost heap (*mired* [2]), the speaker – though exhausted – feels he can

say that he has safely survived to the end of another year. The note here is of relief rather than achievement.

9 **the fugitive in my heart**   that part of my personality that longs for escape.

leaf to leaf   Compare this image with the image of the tree in *Tree at My Window* (page 58).

12 **Now up, my knee**   The poem ends with an image designed to emphasize the effort that will be needed to survive (*to keep on top of*) the coming year. Note that the final image is not of leaves but of snow threatening to overwhelm the speaker.

Neither Out Far nor In Deep

Like *The Sound of Trees* (page 49), *Stopping by Woods on a Snowy Evening* (page 54), *Gathering Leaves* (page 56), and *The Middleness of the Road* (page 70), this poem partly relies for its effect on the apparent simplicity and repetitiveness of its form and rhyme scheme. What effects are created by the use of short lines (usually endstopped – except for lines 7 and 15) and by the succession of very direct statements, culminating in a single question?

There Are Roughly Zones

This poem appears to contain a statement of Frost's pragmatic philosophy of life. It is embedded in a question the speaker asks about why humanity never accepts that there should be limits to human aspirations and expectations:

> Why is his nature forever so hard to teach
> That though there is no fixed line between wrong and right,
> There are roughly zones whose laws must be obeyed?   (11–13)

The irregular long lines and rhyme scheme of the poem suggest a relaxed and almost patient teasing out of the problem, even

while the storm is threatening to ' ...
destroy the peach tree.

3 **the house has long been tried** storms ...
the house many times in the past. It has alw...
survive.

6 **It is very far north, we admit** What point is Fr...
this line? (Look at the last four lines of the poem.)

15 **more than a little betrayed** The speaker and his comp...
unfair that the *northwest wind* (16) should blow so strongly ...
time as the temperature drops so sharply. The tree has little c...
survival.

21 **this limitless trait in the hearts of men** This final line implies tha...
Frost (up to a point at least) approves of the fact that the human spirit...
always wants to go further. There are only *roughly* bounds or *zones* (13)
within which humanity *can stay confined* (8).

from A Witness Tree
The Most of It

By contrast with *There Are Roughly Zones* (page 62) and *Two Look at Two* (page 55) this poem is riddled with anti-climaxes which seem to imply a strong sense of frustration and disappointment. The poem focuses on the figure of an isolated man living beside a lake. He cries out in frustration against the lack of *counter-love, original response* (8) in his life, and, in doing so, he highlights his own loneliness.

As with *The Oven Bird* (page 44), this poem challenges the reader to accept that life seems to give less than it promises. Is this inconsistent with the views apparently expressed in other Frost poems, or does this attitude lie at the heart of his philosophy?

The final statement (*and that was all* [20]) suggests that the title of the poem has to be taken ironically. How do the insistently regular rhyme scheme and iambic metre determine your interpretation of the poem's ending?

5 **To double day** The gleam... lightness of the day. The spea...
consciously aware of the effect its b...

9 **Relying on its beauty** The poem moves...
who see it.

11 **someone reminiscent** The someone who...
imagines a future time in which somebody w...
the young birch when he was *cutting brush along*...
birch has been spared in the same way as the *leap*...
(23) in *The Tuft of Flowers* (page 21).

16 **bole** the stem or trunk of a tree.

19 **And zeal would not be thanked** someone who...
conscientious and cut down the tree would get no t...
else for having done so.

20 **When you were reading books** What is the effe...
you into the poem in line 17 and here? Is the speaker...
himself? In any case, this line seems to suggest that th...
standing as it does, is engaged in an activity just as wo...
reading or travelling.

An Unstamped Letter in Our R... Letter Box

This poem teases in several ways. It is presented in the...
letter addressed to the owner of a property by a tram...
spent the previous night camping in the owner's pastu...
tramp uses strangely formal language (*I elected to de...*
is happy to quote Latin in order to produce a...
couplet. The letter apologizes not for the fact th...
trespassed, but that he might *seem to boast* (3...
of is an experience he had during the ni...
coalesced (26) shot through the sky like...
formed (25), and this prompted a c...
memories in the mind of the speak...
was so powerful that *for a momen*...
thought about in vain (36–7). Wh...

does not say. Indeed, he implies that the owner of the property may well have had similar insights himself. He concludes by suggesting that it was:

> ... partly to compel
> Myself, *in forma pauperis,*
> To say as much I write you this. (50–2)

What other reasons he may have had for writing the letter, again he does not say. If the poem has a moral (and its tone becomes increasingly didactic) it is summed up in the line *Each knows his own discernment best* (43).

Compare the way Frost builds up pairs of contrasts (tramp/scholar, labourer/farm owner, educated/uneducated, etc.) in this poem with other poems where he uses the same technique (e.g. *After Apple-Picking*, page 40). Do you think these contrasts might reflect some of the contradictions Frost is trying to explore in his own personality?

8 **the pip of spades** the ace of spades. The playing-card image is continued in the next line with *a suite of glades* (9).

12 Frost seems to be using the word *demur* here not in its usual sense of 'to make an objection' but to mean 'to stay' (as if from the French *demeurer* – 'to live').

13 **juniper** an evergreen shrub or tree.

26 **coalesced** merged. Having apparently come together to form one star, they went *streaking* (27) (like *molten* metal) through the sky, like a shooting star.

34–5 Why do you think Frost uses sexual images here to describe how the two memories 'coalesce' like the two stars?

38 **my involuntary host** the person to whom the letter is addressed, who had had no say in whether the tramp could spend the night on his property.

42 **Heaven showed your guest** Does this reference to *Heaven* (and the other reference in line 30) suggest that the tramp sees some guiding hand behind the moments of outer and inner illumination he experienced?

51 *in forma pauperis* in the likeness of a pauper or tramp. Does this imply that the speaker is admitting he is not really a tramp at all?

To an Ancient

Reflecting on the discovery of traces of a prehistoric man, Frost is forced to ask the question: will my poetry make it any more likely that I myself shall be remembered in times to come?

2 **The one you made** This refers to the *eolith* (13), presumably a once-standing stone, which has been found *in the delta of a brook* (5). The *delta* is where the brook widens as it runs into a larger river.

10 Archaeologists excavating the human remains of this prehistoric man can estimate his date and discuss his *probable brute nature* (11); however, beyond this nothing about the man can be known – how much more, the poem implies, does one need to know?

13 **eolith** a stone from the eolithic period, which preceded the paleolithic or old stone age. *Eos* (Greek) means 'dawn'.

17 **by using rhyme** i.e. by writing poetry.

18 **I live to lime** i.e. eventually my bones will decay back into earth. *Limus* (Latin) means 'mud'.

The Middleness of the Road

Once again, the theme of this poem is human limitation. The road may seem to go on indefinitely until it disappears into the sky (*The universal blue* [15]) or the woods (*local green* [16]) but the speaker's car is useless except on the road. Frost makes it clear that the sky and the woods for him represent the finality of death (*the absolute flight and rest* [14]). In what ways, therefore, can the poem's title be interpreted?

8 **Fancy** the imagination. Why is the capital letter used?

9 Here the poet is referring to the combustion (*explode*) of the fuel (*mineral drops*) that drives the engine of his car.

from *In the Clearing*

A Cabin in the Clearing

Although many of Frost's poems feature conversation, this is rare in being set out as a scripted dialogue between two speakers. The theme of the poem, that human beings spend much of their lives lost and uncertain but still capable of self-discovery, is central to Frost's work. The key lines are spoken by Smoke:

> If the day ever comes when they know who
> They are, they may know better where they are.   (29–30)

10   **wraith**   ghost.

21–2   If the *Red Man* (21) represents the wisdom of the traditional inhabitants of the place, who is being criticized here – the settlers who (though they *must by now have learned the native tongue* [20]) are not able to understand what is said to them, or the Native American whose message is too obscure?

33   **too sudden to be credible**   *Sudden* here suggests 'recent' or 'new', as if the settlers (the builders of the log cabin) are such newcomers that they cannot yet be taken seriously by those – the guardians of the place – who have always been there.

38   **unrest**   Although the occupants of the cabin are *sleepers* (1), they are unable to rest peacefully because they cannot resolve their *daylong theme* (35). Frost implies that fundamental questions about identity and the meaning of life trouble us all.

40   **the bass from the soprano**   literally, the low note from the high note; here, perhaps, referring both to the voice of a man and a woman and reflecting the deeper and the higher (superficial) problems with which the settlers are having to wrestle. (Compare the *inner haze* [42] and the outer haze.)

For John F. Kennedy His Inauguration

(Gift outright of *The Gift Outright*)

Frost was invited to take part in President Kennedy's inauguration in 1960, an honour that made him in effect the unofficial Poet Laureate of America. He recited from memory his poem *The Gift Outright*, having prefaced it with the couplets that speak optimistically (naively?) about A *golden age of poetry and power* (76).

2 **the august occasions of the state**   formal state ceremonies such as the inauguration of a new president.

4 **my cause**   i.e. poetry.

11 **Colonial**   i.e. in favour of a policy of colonizing the New World discovered by Christopher Columbus at the end of the fifteenth century.

16 France, Spain and the Netherlands had all colonized parts of the New World; gradually they were displaced by *Elizabeth the First and England* (18).

20 **the Latin of our founding sages**   E *Pluribus Unum* – 'Out of Many, One'; the inscription on American dollar bills. Our *founding sages* are the wise men (presidents of the United States) named in lines 25–6.

25–6 **Washington,/John Adams, Jefferson, and Madison**   the *great four* (25) presidents who laid the foundations of the modern United States of America.

27 **consecrated seers**   men with the gift of foresight, who had acquired almost the status of holy leaders.

30 **our Declaration**   the American Declaration of Independence (1776). (See *The Black Cottage*, line 61.)

31 Is this America's goal, or its destiny?

36 **wards**   in legal terms, children for whom someone else (another adult or the courts for example) takes responsibility when their own parents are unable to look after them properly. Here, the reference is to emerging nations of the world who look to the US for protection and support.

46 **the twain**   the Wright brothers, pioneering American aviators.

51 Here Frost is referring to the whole past history of America, which he describes (perhaps tongue-in-cheek) as *revolution and outlawry* – a

mixture of high and low political and social lawlessness.

55 Frost was a strong supporter of John F. Kennedy's campaign for the presidency. He saw Kennedy's election as heralding a new era that would see a return to the idealism of the early American puritan settlers, after the materialism of the Eisenhower presidency (1952–60).

71 **Augustan age**   the golden age of the Roman Empire under Augustus.

The Gift Outright

1 **The land was ours**   Frost claims that America belonged to the Americans (i.e. the American settlers) before they had obtained independence from Great Britain.

4 **Massachusetts, Virginia**   early British colonies on the east coast of America.

12 **we gave ourselves outright**   Note the unconditional submission to the land. This implies not just a complete declaration of loyalty to America as a country, but literally and physically to *the land vaguely realizing westward* (14), the territory that was opened up by the frontiersmen.

The Draft Horse

One of Frost's last poems, *The Draft Horse* is a characteristically unsettling piece of writing. The account of the attack on the horse, delivered in completely unemotional and unembellished tones, is macabre enough; the apparently unquestioning way in which the speaker and his companion accept what has happened leaves the reader feeling disorientated. Is this poem intended to imply that Frost himself believes in a capricious Fate? If so, how would you interpret the buggy and the horse here? Why is the buggy *too frail* (2) and the horse *too heavy* (3)? The pair in the buggy are described as *the least disposed to ascribe/Any more than we had to to hate* (15–16). What does this mean and how does it affect the ending of the poem? In the final stanza, the speaker suggests that the riders will *get down/And walk the rest of the way*

(19–20); why is this a surprising and powerful ending to *The Draft Horse?*

Title **Draft Horse** a large horse used for pulling heavy loads.

12 **one long invidious draft** one straight, indiscriminate swathe, like a ploughed furrow.

Interpretations

One of the features of Frost's poetry that has often been commented on is its 'elusiveness' and the fact that, although it appears simple both in form and content, this simplicity masks a complexity of thought, theme and structure not always apparent on first reading. In fact, his poems contain many layers of meaning and operate on different levels. Looking for a single meaning in one of Frost's poems can sometimes lead to a misunderstanding of what he wants to achieve or convey through the poem.

It can also be limiting to try to interpret Frost's poems in terms of what you know about his life and experiences. There is no doubt that some of his poetry found its starting point in an event, emotion or situation that he experienced, but to try to centre an analysis of a poem on a particular experience would not necessarily be helpful in developing a full appreciation of his work. Nevertheless, it is always useful to keep in mind the context within which Frost was writing. His awareness of the natural environment, and his sense of closeness to the land, is clear in many of his poems, and the majority of his work is set in a rural context.

Themes and ideas

Frost's poetry addresses a variety of themes, but certain ideas crop up repeatedly. Many of his poems explore ideas such as loneliness, isolation and alienation, self-discovery and the need for a man to make the most of his situation. Others deal with love or the breakdown of love, human limitations, and death. His poems cannot be neatly categorized according to theme, however, as they often contain a range of ideas. When reading them you should be alert to various ways in which they can be viewed and interpreted.

The natural world

Although many of Frost's poems use images of nature in a variety of ways and he describes various aspects of nature, such as trees, flowers, the seasons, and landscapes, it is important to understand that nature is not in itself a theme in his poems. He uses ideas and images drawn from the natural world, the landscape, or farms and farming in order to develop and explore his ideas.

A popular and enduring image of Frost is that of the 'farmer poet', but in fact he spent very little of his time on activities connected with farming. During the brief periods in his life when he did farm, he was not particularly successful at it and preferred to take long walks looking at the trees, flowers and wildlife rather than doing the everyday chores involved. There is no doubt, however, that farms played an important part in his life and he did own one for much of his life. The farm seems to have represented for Frost a place of retreat and spiritual renewal.

The Pasture is often regarded as Frost's signature poem, and was the one that he used to preface all the collected and selected editions of his poetry.

Activity

Read *The Pasture* carefully. Why do you think Frost chose the poem to preface the collected and selected editions of his poetry?

Discussion

The farm and the activities necessary to run it are not at the centre of the poem, although the speaker describes his intention to go about the chores that are typical of the tasks to be done on a farm – cleaning the *pasture spring* (1), raking away the leaves, waiting to check that the water runs clear.

The second stanza introduces the idea of the speaker tending to a calf that is *so young* it is unsteady on its legs. The repetition of *I shan't be gone long* in the final line of each stanza suggests that the demands of the farm are taking him away from someone (or something) that he wants to return to. The invitation *You come too* perhaps invites this person to join him, but also offers the reader the chance to share the experience through the power of the poetic imagination.

Two more poems in which Frost uses activities on the farm as the starting point are *Mowing* and *The Tuft of Flowers*.

Activity

Compare the style and tone of *Mowing* and *The Tuft of Flowers* and consider how Frost uses these two poems to present his ideas.

Discussion

Mowing is written in the form of a sonnet, and takes as its starting point images of the speaker mowing the grass with a scythe. The use of the first person (*I* and *my*) creates a sense of directness and a tone of intimacy, as if the speaker is sharing some important truth with the reader. This sense of an intimate tone is emphasized through the repetition of *whispering* (2) and *whispered* (3, 14).

The contemplative tone is further sustained through the questions that the speaker poses to himself throughout the poem, as his thoughts combine the sights and sensations of nature – *the heat of the sun* (4), the *feeble-pointed spikes of flowers* (11), and the *hay to make* (14) – with the sense of something magical. The speaker's scythe *whispering to the ground* (2) creates both a sense of connectedness between the speaker and the environment and also a feeling of mystery as he poses the question *What was it it whispered?* (3) – a question to which the speaker does not know the answer. The speaker's thoughts delve deeper and deeper into the question, offering possible answers:

> Perhaps it was something about the heat of the sun,
> Something, perhaps, about the lack of sound –
> And that was why it whispered and did not speak.
>
> (4–6)

This leads him to the paradox that:

> Anything more than the truth would have seemed too weak
> To the earnest love that laid the swale in rows
>
> (9–10)

The respect inherent in the relationship between the mower and nature acknowledges truth, not an embellishment of it. For, as the penultimate line asserts: *The fact is the sweetest dream that labor knows.* The final line brings the poem full circle with the repetition of the whispering of the scythe.

In *The Tuft of Flowers* Frost also uses the first person, and again the speaker is carrying out a typical farm task – turning the grass when it is drying in the sun after being mown. In contrast to the sonnet form of *Mowing*, *The Tuft of Flowers* is written in 20 rhyming couplets, most of which are end-stopped. This gives the poem a certain insistent rhythm suggestive of an older style of poetic writing. This sense is emphasized further by:

- the use of archaic vocabulary, such as *o'er* (13), *thus* (25), *henceforth* (34)
- inversion of word order, such as *swift there passed me by* (11), *I worked no more alone* (34)
- the repetitive effect of the rhymes, such as *heart* (39) and *apart* (40), and the repetition of *alone* (8, 34) and *ground* (16, 32).

The sense of the past evoked by the formality of the archaic style perhaps adds to a sense of the timelessness of the interaction between humanity and nature. In *Mowing*, the speaker is captivated by the activity and the sound of his scythe as it cuts through the grass. In *The Tuft of Flowers* the speaker, turning the grass, thinks about the person who mowed it in the first place, but he is nowhere to be seen or heard and the speaker is alone. This sense of loneliness holds more significance, however:

> But he had gone his way, the grass all mown,
> And I must be, as he had been – alone,
>
> 'As all must be,' I said within my heart,
> 'Whether they work together or apart.'

(7–10)

This moves the poem on from the specific loneliness of the speaker or the mower to the universal loneliness that is a part of the human condition.

Immediately, however, the speaker's thoughts are distracted by a butterfly seeking *Some resting flower of yesterday's delight* (14). Questions arise in the speaker's mind as the butterfly searches far and wide before finding *a tall tuft of flowers beside a brook,/ A leaping tongue of bloom the scythe had spared* (22–23). The butterfly leads the speaker's eye to this sight and also leads him to a recognition that the mower had spared the flowers because he had loved them. This causes the speaker to feel a bond with the mower in sharing an appreciation for the beauty of the flowers, and his sense of loneliness is dispelled. He now hears, in his imagination, the mower's *long scythe whispering to the ground* (32) – note the connection with the poem *Mowing* through the image of the whispering scythe. The butterfly has led the speaker's eye to a sight whose *leaping tongue of bloom* brings him a *message from the dawn* (30). Note the many references to time in the poem, and the sense that the speaker is separated from the mower by time. This *message* from an earlier time makes him *feel a spirit kindred to my own* and dispels the sense of isolation, *So that henceforth I worked no more alone* (33–34.) He ends with the realization that work brings people together in a sense of common purpose and humanity, *Whether they work together or apart* (40).

Many aspects of nature feature repeatedly in Frost's poetry, and the notion of the cycle of nature and of life is a theme he returns to again and again. One aspect of nature that was particularly important to Frost was that of trees and leaves, both of which are important symbols in a number of his poems.

Activity

Look at *In Hardwood Groves*, *Gathering Leaves* and *A Leaf-Treader*. How does Frost use the image of leaves to explore his ideas in these poems?

Discussion

The title of *In Hardwood Groves* tells us a good deal. The poet is describing a grove of trees – the fact that they are hardwood trees means that they shed their leaves in the autumn. Immediately the opening lines of the poem create a strong sense of the cycle of nature being repeated endlessly: *The same leaves over and over again!* (1). The phrase *The same leaves* emphasizes the fact that this

Trees and leaves are important symbols in Frost's poetry

process is replicated year after year as winter approaches. This is part of the natural cycle of life, and the fallen leaves *fit the earth like a leather glove* (4). The leaves must wither, fall and decay before new life and new leaves emerge in the spring. The new life and the old are both part of one process, and one cannot exist without the other. Notice the repeated *They must* (7, 8), which emphasizes the natural order of things – this is the way it is and this is the way it must be in our world, the speaker concludes:

> However it is in some other world
> I know that this is the way in ours.

(11–12)

In *Gathering Leaves* the speaker describes the gathering up of fallen leaves in autumn. In the first three stanzas he gives a description of the physical process of collecting the leaves: the way that spades are not very good at shovelling them up, the lightness of the bags full of leaves, the rustling sound they make, *Like rabbit and deer/ Running away* (7–8). He describes the way in which, when he tries to pick up the *mountains* of leaves he has created, they:

Elude my embrace,
Flowing over my arms
And into my face.

(10–12)

He then describes all the work he has put in, how he:

may load and unload
Again and again
Till I fill the whole shed

(13–15)

This leads up to the key question of the poem: *And what have I then?* (16). He is raising the question of how we put a value on work done. The leaves have no weight, no colour, and are of little use – *But a crop is a crop* (22). In their own way the gathered leaves are a kind of harvest:

And who's to say where
The harvest shall stop?

(23–24)

The tightly structured verse form, with short, mostly five-syllable lines and simple rhyme pattern, gives *Gathering Leaves* a sense of the vigour of the physical effort involved in the task described, which is in contrast to *A Leaf-Treader*. Here the speaker is weary after a day of treading down the leaves for composting, and this sense of weariness is reflected in the long, slow pace of the lines. There is a feeling that much, perhaps too much energy has been expended on the task and the ideas of fear and (lack of) safety are introduced, giving a slightly sinister edge to the poem and raising some questions. Why has he been *too fierce from fear* (3)? Why does he choose the word *safely* to describe how the leaves have been dealt with (4)? Like the speaker in *In Hardwood Groves*, the speaker here thinks of the leaves when they were overhead on the trees, but this thought brings no comfort, and instead the sense of menace is reaffirmed:

All summer long I thought I heard them threatening under their
breath.
And when they came it seemed with a will to carry me with them
to death.

(7–8)

The final stanza reveals that this thought does have some attraction, as:

They spoke to the fugitive in my heart as if it were leaf to leaf.
They tapped at my eyelids and touched my lips with an invitation
to grief.

(9–10)

Part of the speaker's mind, the part that wants to escape from life,
seems tempted by this possibility and some critics have compared this

Robert Frost in woods in 1961

poem to *Stopping by Woods on a Snowy Evening*, where *The woods are lovely, dark, and deep* (13) and seem to lure him into their darkness. In both poems, however, he resists the temptation and resolves to carry on with the tasks of life, although the final line: *Now up, my knee, to keep on top of another year of snow* (12) makes it clear that coping with another year will not be achieved without effort.

Several of Frost's poems have trees as a central image, but normally the speaker is out of doors observing and experiencing the sights and sounds of nature. In *Tree at My Window*, however, the speaker is indoors looking out of his window at a tree. His window is closed but the curtains are not drawn, as he does not want to be cut off from the tree.

Activity

How does Frost achieve his effects in *Tree at My Window*?

Discussion

Unlike poems such as *Birches*, where trees give rise to a meditation of some kind, here the speaker addresses the tree directly:

> But let there never be curtain drawn
> Between you and me.
>
> (3–4)

He does not see the tree as the possessor of inherent wisdom (7–8), but the imagery he uses to describe it is striking and full of respect for the tree:

> Vague dream-head lifted out of the ground,
> And thing next most diffuse to cloud,
> Not all your light tongues talking aloud
> Could be profound.
>
> (5–8)

The *But* that opens the third stanza signals, however, that although the *light tongues* (7) of the tree could not be *profound* (8), he and the tree share something. He has seen the tree *taken and tossed* (9) and imagines how the tree has seen him *when I was taken and swept/ And all but lost* (11–12). In this sense, he feels a shared identity with the tree and sees it as a fellow sufferer; metaphorically, in the tree he sees himself.

In the final stanza, he again uses personification, this time of *Fate*, reflecting on the way she brought them together, but recognizing the key difference between them as the speaker grapples with his own fears and doubts about life:

> Your head so much concerned with outer,
> Mine with inner, weather.

(15–16)

The structure of this poem, in four quatrains using an *abba* rhyme scheme, appears to bring a certain regularity to it, but the rhythm patterns vary and, coupled with the short fourth line of each quatrain, this creates a noticeable variation of tone as the poem develops.

Activity

Now look at *Desert Places*. How do the ideas explored here compare with those in *Tree at My Window*?

Discussion

In *Desert Places* the speaker describes snow falling as night approaches. Notice the emphasis and the sense of urgency created by the repetition and alliteration of the words *falling* and *fast* in the first line: *Snow falling and night falling fast, oh, fast*.

The scene has a sense of increasing emptiness about it as the snow covers the field, leaving only, for the moment, *a few weeds and stubble showing last* (4). Soon all will be covered by the snow.

The field now appears to be part of the woods that surround it: they *have it – it is theirs* (5). The covering snow has taken away all boundaries to create one unified landscape, but it is a landscape devoid of life, and *All animals are smothered in their lairs* (6). The speaker's own spirit reflects the sense of isolation and loneliness evoked by the scene:

> I am too absent-spirited to count;
> The loneliness includes me unawares.

(7–8)

Frost creates images of snowy landscapes in several poems

The third stanza picks up the word *loneliness* from the final line of the second stanza, and the idea of loneliness is repeated twice more (9, 10). This reinforces the speaker's own feelings of isolation and adds further to the sense that it will grow worse before it gets better, and will bring:

> A blanker whiteness of benighted snow
> With no expression, nothing to express.
>
> (11–12)

In the final stanza the speaker expresses a defiant attitude to this scene of loneliness that has been evoked through the images of the snow. He is prepared to face his fears of loneliness and isolation, but he asserts that these fears were not created by the falling snow, nor by the *empty spaces/ Between stars – on stars where no human race is* (13–14). Like the fears and uncertainties he expresses in *Tree at My Window*, these are created within his own mind:

I have it in me so much nearer home
To scare myself with my own desert places.

(15–16)

As in *Tree at My Window*, in *Desert Places* the exterior world, this time
of snow falling on a landscape, mirrors the speaker's feelings and his
fears of isolation and alienation, and causes him to face them.

Snow was the source of important images for Frost and he uses
these in many of his poems, including perhaps his most famous
one, *Stopping by Woods on a Snowy Evening*. The poem appears
deceptively simple. The title gives a precise and clear summary of
the event it describes: the speaker pauses near some woods as night
falls and he watches the snow falling and filling up the woods.

Activity

Look carefully at *Stopping by Woods on a Snowy Evening*. What
meanings do you think it holds beyond the apparently simple
description of an event?

Discussion

Like so many of Frost's poems, this takes as its starting point an
observation of the natural world. Note here how the speaker appears
to be between the natural wilderness of the woods and the world of
humanity, represented by the village where the owner of the woods
lives:

Whose woods these are I think I know.
His house is in the village, though;
He will not see me stopping here
To watch his woods fill up with snow.

(1–4)

These lines suggest something secretive and unusual about the
speaker's behaviour; he is doing something alone, unobserved, away
from civilization, *without a farmhouse near* (6) on the *darkest
evening of the year* (8).

Despite the apparent tranquillity of the scene, the poem seems to hold a darkness; not just the literal darkness of the woods or of the darkest night of the year, but the metaphorical darkness that this implies. Some critics have suggested that the poem is really a meditation on death, perhaps even suicide. The darkness of the woods tempts the speaker – they are *lovely, dark, and deep* (13) – but the combination of woods, darkness and snow suggests that their seductive attractiveness masks the danger of becoming lost.

Certainly the final stanza indicates that the speaker feels he faces a dilemma that necessitates making a choice. Some readers have seen this as the speaker choosing to go on with life; he has commitments (*promises to keep*, 14), and much still to achieve – *miles to go* (15, 16) – before he can rest. Some have seen the repetition of this final line as the speaker affirming his decision to resist the temptation to be drawn away from society, or from life. Others have read this as expressing indecision about the choice.

Another view of the poem emphasizes the importance of its form. Like the content of the poem, this has a complexity that is belied by a superficial simplicity. Note, for example, that the third, unrhyming line from each of the first three stanzas provides the rhyming sound for each succeeding stanza, and in the final stanza all the lines rhyme. Its interlocking rhyme scheme and metrical patterning are often overlooked in the search for 'meaning' in the poem.

Philosophy and meditations

Birches is one of Frost's most well-known and popular poems, and like a number of his other poems uses images of trees. The poem has been viewed as expressing Frost's philosophical outlook as well as marking a change in his development as a poet.

Activity
Read *Birches* carefully. What do you notice about how Frost creates his effects here?

Discussion

One of the first things you may notice about the poem is its striking combination of imagery and naturalistic description.

The poem opens with a description of birches bent *to left and right* and this gives rise, in the speaker's mind's eye, to the image of a boy swinging on them. The image of the boy is quickly dismissed and replaced by the real reason for the bent branches – ice. However, establishing the image of the boy playing at the outset of the poem is important, as the poet will return to it later in the poem.

Having established that the bending of the trees was caused by an ice storm and not a boy at play, the poem goes on to a beautifully descriptive passage that contains a closely observed depiction of the birches bending under the weight of ice after an ice storm:

> Often you must have seen them
> Loaded with ice a sunny winter morning
> After a rain. They click upon themselves
> As the breeze rises, and turn many-colored
> As the stir cracks and crazes their enamel.
>
> (5–9)

This beauty is transitory, as the stir of the breeze *cracks and crazes their enamel* (9) and the sun melts them and *makes them shed crystal shells* (10). Note the hint of destruction here, with the words *Shattering* and *heaps of broken glass* (11, 12) followed by the image *You'd think the inner dome of heaven had fallen* (13) and the description of the branches being *dragged to the withered bracken by the load* (14).

This section of the poem concludes with a striking simile comparing the arching trunks and trailing boughs to girls on all fours with their hair thrown forward, drying in the sun.

The speaker returns to his original thoughts about a boy being the cause of the bent branches. Note the more prosaic language he uses to speak of the *Truth* (21) interrupting his thoughts about the boy. It has been suggested that the following section describing the boy playing in the trees could be a metaphor for Frost's career, and the speaker explicitly links himself with the boy here:

So was I once myself a swinger of birches.
And so I dream of going back to be.

(41–42)

Notice how the personal voice has now become dominant in the poem – the *I* has replaced the *he*.

The speaker dreams of going back to being a boy, a *swinger of birches* (41), perhaps suggesting a desire to escape from the real, adult world into the world of the imagination. The speaker suggests that when weary of the realities of life he wants to *get away from earth awhile* (48) and then come back to it refreshed and ready to begin again.

The final lines of the poem return to the metaphor of the *swinger of birches*, with the speaker imagining himself climbing **Toward** *heaven, till the tree could bear no more* (56) and then being set down on the ground again by the branches. Both the escape into the world of the imagination and the return to reality would have their own rewards; it *would be good both going and coming back* (58).

Activity

What ideas do you think *Birches* draws attention to, and what does it reveal about Frost's 'philosophy'?

Discussion

Some critics have seen the poem as exploring a deepening of the poet's self-awareness, through the metaphor of the discovery of the bent branches of the birches, and the thoughts and reflections that this discovery triggers. Part, at least, of this self-awareness acknowledges that there are times in the poet's life when he needs to withdraw from the world and escape into the life of the spirit or the imagination, in order to be able to return to everyday life spiritually refreshed.

On one level Frost sees the imagination as having the power to transcend the limitations of the real world. However, he also seems to say that complete escape into the world of the imagination is neither possible nor desirable, although it provides comfort when:

life is too much like a pathless wood
Where your face burns and tickles with the cobwebs

> Broken across it, and one eye is weeping
> From a twig's having lashed across it open.
>
> (44–47)

Some have seen the poem as exploring the idea that the world in which we live has limits, sometimes self-imposed, and sometimes imposed by external factors. Frost recognizes that the removal of limits is neither possible nor desirable. Earth is the place where love exists (52), and to escape from the earth would be to deprive oneself of love.

Other readings of the poem extend the idea further and explore the notion that by attempting to push these boundaries, the poetic imagination allows the poet to assert his individuality and in so doing transcend the limitations of the everyday world.

After Apple-Picking takes as its starting point another farm activity and, like *Birches*, uses it to explore his ideas on the nature of life.

Activity

Examine how Frost presents his ideas in *After Apple-Picking*.

Discussion

In *After Apple-Picking* Frost adopts the first-person voice to express the thoughts of a speaker who is on the verge of falling asleep after a hard day working on the farm. The visual images he uses are all drawn from farm work: the ladder propped against the apple tree, the ice at the water trough, the *load on load of apples coming in* (26). Notice Frost's appeal to various senses here: *The scent of the apples* (8), *every fleck of russet showing clear* (20), and the *pressure* of the ladder rungs still on his feet (22). The images, however, are distorted and run together as the speaker's tired mind hovers on the edge of sleep. At the end of the poem the speaker thinks about the nature of the sleep he is about to experience and whether it will be *just some human sleep* (42) or will be like the hibernation sleep of the woodchuck – perhaps suggesting death.

Like many other Frost poems, this begins with a description of everyday events and scenes on the farm but, through the everyday situation, the poet is led to consider the deepest questions of human existence. These are developed here through the relationship between the activity and its satisfactions and the consequent exhaustion it involves. Although a task such as picking apples has its pleasures, it also has imperfections and frustrations, because complete fulfilment is never achieved: *there's a barrel that I didn't fill* (3) and there are *Apples I didn't pick* (5); some apples fall and are bruised. Notice too the stress placed on the daunting scale of the work: *There were ten thousand thousand fruit to touch* (30). This is an activity that he seeks and welcomes, yet which exhausts him and leaves him more concerned with its failures than its successes. His final questioning of the nature of the sleep that is about to overwhelm him perhaps symbolizes the uncertainties that he feels lie ahead.

Activity

The language of *After Apple-Picking* reinforces a sense of the contradictions in life. Look at the poem again and pick out examples of Frost's use of contrasts.

Discussion

Examples of the contrasts created include the following.
- Summer is contrasted with winter – the late summer harvest time also brings the *Essence of winter sleep* (7) and ice that has to be scooped from the drinking trough, which is held against *hoary grass* (12).
- The necessity of the work and the pleasure it brings are contrasted with the exhaustion it causes – *I have had too much/ Of apple-picking: I am overtired/ Of the great harvest I myself desired* (27–29).
- The satisfaction of completing the task is contrasted with the disappointment that in some senses it remains unfulfilled – there is the overwhelming quantity of *fruit to touch,/ Cherish in hand* (30–31), the *barrel that I didn't fill* (3), the *Apples I didn't pick* (5).
- The wakefulness of the working hours is contrasted with the impending sleep.

Some have seen this poem as presenting Frost's feelings about his poetry, and have suggested that it depicts the satisfaction that writing poetry has given him even though the intensity of his imaginative activity has drained him. The harvest has been a full one, but there are also failures and unfulfilled potential. The question that the poem leaves with the reader is: What is the nature of the sleep he goes to, and what lies beyond it?

Like *Birches*, *The Wood-Pile* also takes as its starting point a discovery made while out walking, and as in *After Apple-Picking* an apparently insignificant incident creates a vivid experience in the speaker's mind.

Activity

Look at *The Wood-Pile*. What ideas do you think Frost explores here?

Discussion

The poem begins with a sense of purposelessness, and the speaker seems undecided whether to turn back or go on. The poem is permeated with a feeling of decay and gloom, established from the opening line describing the *frozen swamp* and the *gray day*. The reference to the *frozen swamp* perhaps brings to mind Frost's attempted escape to the 'Great Dismal Swamp' before his marriage, from which he returned with a new determination for life (see page 3).

The speaker here is distracted momentarily by a small bird alighting close by, and then he discovers the wood-pile, his eye led to it by the bird.

The significant thing about the wood-pile is that it has clearly been created for a purpose, but now appears abandoned:

> It was a cord of maple, cut and split
> And piled – and measured, four by four by eight.
> And not another like it could I see.
> No runner tracks in this year's snow looped near it.
> And it was older sure than this year's cutting,
> Or even last year's or the year's before.
> The wood was gray and the bark warping off it
> And the pile somewhat shrunken.

(23–30)

This sight causes him to reflect on the nature of the person who had created the wood-pile, and:

> I thought that only
> Someone who lived in turning to fresh tasks
> Could so forget his handiwork on which
> He spent himself

(34–37)

The task had been completed but the purpose of the task, the use of the logs on a fire, remained unfulfilled. The final line ends the poem on the dismal note on which it started: *With the slow smokeless burning of decay.*

The speaker seems alone and isolated, surrounded by nature but lost and confused. The only sign of life is the bird that leads him to the wood-pile. Although great care and effort had been expended in the creation of the wood-pile it is now decaying, perhaps suggesting that in the context of the natural world the effect of our work, as well as that of our lives, is merely temporary.

In one of Frost's most famous poems, *The Road Not Taken*, another apparently trivial experience gives rise to a meditation on the nature of existence. The poem seems on the surface quite simple, but interpretations of it have varied considerably. Many interpretations take the poem as encouraging the individual to go his or her own way, and not to be afraid to take a road *less traveled by*.

Activity

Look carefully at *The Road Not Taken*. Do you notice any contradictions in this poem?

Discussion

The title of the poem refers to the option that the speaker did not take, but the key focus of the poem is the road he does take – *the one less traveled by* (19). Immediately, though, there appears to be a contradiction in that both roads are described as equally well travelled – *the passing there/ Had worn them really about the same* (9–10) – although the lines before tell us that one road had *perhaps the better claim,/ Because it was grassy and wanted wear* (7–8).

Further contradictions follow. The speaker exclaims *Oh, I kept the first for another day!* (13), yet he is well aware that taking one path leads to another and *I doubted if I should ever come back* (15). This suggests that the choice, although apparently of little consequence, is in fact one that will shape all his future options.

The final stanza begins with the speaker predicting that he will be *telling this with a sigh/ Somewhere ages and ages hence* (16–17). Again this suggests that the decision being taken is an important one, and the *sigh* perhaps expresses regret, over the option not taken and the opportunity missed.

Frost's own account of how *The Road Not Taken* came to be written, and what sparked the idea for it, tells us that in 1914 he was with his wife Elinor, Edward Thomas and Thomas's wife Helen gathered round a log fire one night in a farmhouse in Gloucestershire. They had just heard that war had been declared, and Edward Thomas first felt that he should join up straight away, but then thought that perhaps he should wait a little while. Frost explains that Thomas was always careful when he had to make a decision, weighing things up for a long time before choosing what he would do. Frost commented that: 'the poem came less from me than from him'.

On closer analysis the idea that the poem encourages others to do as the speaker did and go their own way, not following the crowd but taking a less common path, seems much less secure. It is, perhaps, more a meditation on the way in which some decisions become irrevocable and on the crucial nature of choices that people must make at certain key points in their lives.

Frost's friendship with Edward Thomas was very important to him (see page 7). Thomas's death in the Battle of Arras in April 1917 was a loss deeply felt by Frost and it inspired the poem which, through its title *To E.T.*, he dedicated to Thomas.

Edward Thomas in 1914

Activity

Compare the way Frost explores his ideas in *To E.T.* and *A Soldier*.

Discussion

To E.T. is addressed directly to Thomas, and the speaker begins by describing the way he had fallen asleep while reading Thomas's poetry:

> I slumbered with your poems on my breast,
> Spread open as I dropped them half-read through
> Like dove wings on a figure on a tomb

(1–3)

Note the effect of the simile here – the open leaves of the volume spread like *dove wings*, the symbol of peace, *on my breast*, which becomes a *tomb*.

The speaker thinks about missed opportunities, and how he now cannot speak to Thomas and call him:

First soldier, and then poet, and then both,
Who died a soldier-poet of your race.

(7–8)

The third stanza contains a very personal address to Thomas, as *brother*, and describes the two men's wish *that nothing should remain/ Unsaid* between them. He refers to one more thing that had not been said because it *was not then to say:/ The Victory for what it lost and gained* (11–12). The meaning of this is not entirely clear, although the central irony is evident. Frost could not have said then, when Thomas was alive to hear it, what he is saying now, through this poem, because it is Thomas's death that has given rise to the poem.

The fourth stanza describes the way in which Thomas met his death on Vimy Ridge and how with his death *The war seemed over more for you than me,/ But now for me than you – the other way* (15–16). There is a reference to the continued threat posed by Germany even after the end of the First World War, when the *foe* was *thrust back unsafe beyond the Rhine* (18).

The poem ends with the speaker wondering how the war can truly be over when he cannot speak of it to Thomas, and please him once more with his words. This is perhaps a reference to Thomas's favourable reviews of Frost's poetry. The poem ends, then, with a sense of profound loss – the loss of his friend and the loss of that friend's support and approval for his work.

In *A Soldier* Frost uses the sonnet form and a more formal tone, and the poem is not about a particular individual; the soldier here becomes a universal symbol. The poem opens with a striking image in which the soldier is represented by his *fallen lance that lies as hurled,/ That lies unlifted now, come dew, come rust.* The speaker goes on to reflect on the fact that, if the lance does not appear to have found a worthy target, the death of the soldier will appear pointless:

It is because like men we look too near,
Forgetting that as fitted to the sphere,
Our missiles always make too short an arc.

(6-8)

His thoughts are broadened here to consider how, in life, human beings often take too limited a view. However, the sacrifice of the soldier cannot be measured in terms of ordinary human endeavours, and through his death his spirit was released from the limitations of earthly existence:

> But this we know, the obstacle that checked
> And tripped the body, shot the spirit on
> Further than target ever showed or shone.

(12–14)

Narrative voice

All of Frost's poems present a narrative in their own ways, but in his longer poems the dramatic situation and narrative personas he creates become important elements in the overall effect of the poem. For example, *Home Burial* is written in a 'dramatic' style exploring, largely through dialogue, the relationship between a husband and wife whose young son has died. The poem presents the tensions this has caused between the couple, leading to bitter exchanges and a breakdown in communication and their marriage.

Activity

How does Frost present and dramatize the scene in *Home Burial*? Do you think the poem contains any messages beyond the dramatic situation it portrays?

Discussion

Here are some ideas you may have thought of.

The poem is written in blank verse, often said to be the verse form that most closely resembles the rhythm patterns of natural speech in English. This allows Frost to create the sense of realistic speech within a poetic framework. The convincing naturalness of the dialogue makes it easy to overlook the fact that lines such as these follow the metrical pattern of blank verse:

> 'There you go sneering now!'
>   'I'm not, I'm not!
> You make me angry. I'll come down to you.
> God, what a woman! And it's come to this,
> A man can't speak of his own child that's dead.'

(67–70)

The third-person narrative that comes between the sections of dialogue adopts an impersonal stance and serves to give the reader an impression of the movement and gestures of the man and woman, and so to underline the tension created through the dialogue. For example:

> He spoke
> Advancing towards her: 'What is it you see
> From up there always? – for I want to know.'
> She turned and sank upon her skirts at that,
> And her face changed from terrified to dull.

(5–9)

The dialogue itself is convincing not only in its speech patterns but in its content. For example, *'What is it – what?' she said./ 'Just that I see'* (18), and:

> 'Can't a man speak of his own child he's lost?'
>
> 'Not you – Oh, where's my hat? Oh, I don't need it!
> I must get out of here. I must get air. –
> I don't know rightly whether any man can'.
>
> 'Amy! Don't go to someone else this time...'

(35–39)

These lines create a sense of the tension and stifling grief of the mother as she becomes increasingly unable to cope with her loss, and the husband's apparently stoical response. His words underline the gulf between them as he is unable to express his feelings and is not unwilling but unable to offer words that may help and comfort her.

The poem presents a very painful picture of the grief of the mother and father, but the sadness goes beyond the pain of the loss of a child. There is a double tragedy here – the loss of a son and the disintegration of a marriage. The poem shows that both the mother and the father are grieving in their own ways, but neither can understand the other, nor can they communicate the way they feel to each other. The wife misinterprets her husband's attitude – the way he copes by dealing with the practicalities of death, such as digging the grave himself – taking it to show lack of feeling. He, on the other hand, does not know how to cope with his wife's grief, which manifests itself in complete despair, the feeling she is cursed and that the world is evil.

The poem therefore explores human feelings and responses to the death of a loved one and the different coping mechanisms they use to try to bear the grief.

Although again telling a story through narrative and dialogue, *The Death of the Hired Man* is very different from *Home Burial*. In this poem, Mary tries to persuade Warren, her husband, to take back an old farmhand who has let them down in the past. Silas, the farmhand, is old and ill. Mary believes he has returned to the only place he knows as 'home'. When Mary finally persuades Warren to take him back, they find the old man has died.

Activity

What does the narrative poem *The Death of the Hired Man* have in common with *Home Burial*, and in what ways is it different?

Discussion

Like *Home Burial* the poem is set in a rural environment, but in *The Death of the Hired Man* the references to the activities and tasks involved in running a farm are much more overt. The poem, again like *Home Burial*, uses the blank verse form, a third-person narrator and dialogue between a husband and wife. Again, a death is at the heart of the poem. However, the context here is in stark contrast to that of *Home Burial*; although there is a clear difference of view between Warren and Mary, there is also genuine communication and her compassion and willingness to help Silas overcome Warren's feelings of resentment at being let down by Silas in the past.

When Mary tells her husband that Silas *has come home to die* (111) her husband repeats the word *home* in a mocking way, but this is tempered by the modifier *gently*. Her compassionate response to the situation is contrasted to Warren's rational, hard-headed view: *'Home is the place where, when you have to go there,/ They have to take you in'* (118–119). But in the end he does go to talk to Silas.

It is one of the ironies of the poem that, despite returning to the farm to die among those who have shown him kindness in the past, Silas in fact dies alone.

One of the things that Frost wanted to achieve in his poetry was to speak in a simple and genuine language, in the kind of poetic language that William Wordsworth called 'a man speaking to men'. In his biography of Frost, William H. Pritchard (see Further Reading, page 157) points out (page 92):

> If variety is felt in the different forms Frost used and in the different ways of tale telling within these forms, it is also there in the poems' diction. Although he spoke as if the level of diction were uniform ('I have dropped to an everyday level of diction that even Wordsworth kept above'), a language 'absolutely unliterary'… his actual practice was not at all so uniform. This can be seen by comparing the 'unliterary' parts of certain poems with other, heightened moments in them where the diction rises to express a passionate feeling which momentarily surfaces. Edward Thomas had seen as much when he pointed out how the language ranges from the colloquial to 'brief moments of heightened and intense simplicity'.

This is clearly illustrated in *The Black Cottage*, which tells the story of an old woman whose husband had been killed in the Civil War. Her sons have moved away, and when she dies the cottage and everything in it is left as it has always been.

Activity

What do you notice about the form of narration Frost uses in *The Black Cottage*?

Discussion

There are two characters in the poem – a minister is showing around the other, unnamed character. The minister relates the story of the old woman to this unnamed character who, in turn, is relating the tale to the reader. The unnamed character gives a first-person account of this experience interspersed with direct speech from the minister.

At some points, the minister digresses from his main story in what seems a trivial, perhaps tedious, way. For example, here he talks of the old woman's late husband:

He fell at Gettysburg or Fredericksburg,
I ought to know – it makes a difference which:
Fredericksburg wasn't Gettysburg, of course.
But what I'm getting to is how forsaken
A little cottage this has always seemed

(31–35)

This kind of narration can be seen as casual or long-winded, but it can also be argued that it creates realistic dialogue. Pritchard points out that Frost's 'purpose is importantly served by such "digressive" moments which, when broken out of – as the minister eventually does here – enhance the actuality and intimacy of the art, though they may try our patience in the process' (page 97).

When the minister returns to his subject – the old woman and her attendance at his church services – he recounts to his listener how, as a concession to the younger members of his congregation, he would have made a slight alteration to the Creed by removing the phrase *'descended into Hades'* (94), which *seemed too pagan to our liberal youth* (95). He decided not to, though, for fear that the old woman would miss it from the Creed, *As a child misses the unsaid Good-night/ And falls asleep with heartache* (102–103).

The minister continues in his homely, colloquial style:

I'm just as glad she made me keep hands off,
For, dear me, why abandon a belief
Merely because it ceases to be true.

(104–106)

From this simple, personal and colloquial style the minister's language becomes heightened and rises to express a passionate feeling that is not at all the 'absolutely unliterary' language Frost had spoken of. The minister wishes he could avoid unwelcome change by becoming *monarch of a desert land*:

> So desert it would have to be, so walled
> By mountain ranges half in summer snow,
> No one would covet it or think it worth
> The pains of conquering to force change on.
> Scattered oases where men dwelt, but mostly
> Sand dunes held loosely in tamarisk
> Blown over and over themselves in idleness.
> Sand grains should sugar in the natal dew
> The babe born to the desert, the sandstorm
> Retard mid-waste my cowering caravans –

(115–124)

Almost in mid-flow the minister breaks off, and the language of the poem switches again to capture an image that ends the poem on one of the 'brief moments of heightened and intense simplicity' spoken of by Thomas:

> 'There are bees in this wall.' He struck the clapboards,
> Fierce heads looked out; small bodies pivoted.
> We rose to go. Sunset blazed on the windows.

(125–127)

Frost presents a rather different kind of narrative in 'Out, Out –'. The title of the poem comes from a line in a soliloquy by Macbeth, about how brief and pointless life can seem, which gives a good indication of Frost's theme here. The poem describes a farm accident that is both shocking and tragic in its consequences.

Activity

How does Frost develop his narrative in *'Out, Out –'*?

Discussion

The narrator describes the scene and events in the voice of an observer viewing things dispassionately and objectively, except for simply expressing a wish that things had been done differently (line 10). Again blank verse is used to create a sense of the natural rhythms of speech, an effect reinforced by the simple, everyday vocabulary.

The opening nine lines set the scene of the poem in terms of both activity and location. The first line creates an impression of the characteristic sound of the buzz saw – a sound that immediately creates a sense of menace, and which is repeated twice in line 7: *The buzz saw snarled and rattled in the yard.* The activity is set in a physical context by the *Five mountain ranges one behind the other/ Under the sunset far into Vermont* (5–6). The repeated phrase *snarled and rattled* (1, 7) reflects the repeated action of the sawing of the wood and the changes in the engine note that this creates.

The boy is introduced – but he is unnamed. It is the end of the day, and an ominous note is introduced as the narrator expresses the wish that they had *Call[ed] it a day* earlier (10). If this had been done, the boy would have been saved. Ironically, it is at the instant when the boy's sister calls *'Supper'* that the saw leaps out of the boy's hand and the accident occurs (14). Note how the saw, already described as if it were an animal *snarling*, is described as if alive in a simile:

> At the word, the saw,
> As if to prove saws knew what supper meant,
> Leapt out at the boy's hand, or seemed to leap –

> (14–16)

The boy's shock at his terrible injury is clear in his incongruous response, *a rueful laugh*, and the image of him as:

> he swung toward them holding up the hand,
> Half in appeal, but half as if to keep
> The life from spilling.

> (20–22)

Realization of what has happened hits the boy and *He saw all spoiled* (25). His plea to his sister to save his hand is futile, and the simple comment of the narrator – *So. But the hand was gone already* (27) – has all the more impact because of its detached and neutral tone.

The second shock of the poem, the death of the boy, is delivered swiftly in the last four lines. Again the narrative voice is impersonal and matter-of-fact, and the ending is abrupt:

> They listened at his heart.
> Little – less – nothing! – and that ended it.
> No more to be build on there. And they, since they
> Were not the one dead, turned to their affairs.

(31–34)

The lack of emotional response to this tragedy is striking. However, it perhaps also reveals a stoicism and acceptance that since there is nothing more to be done, life must go on, and the work of the farm must be attended to.

Activity

Look again at *'Out, Out –'*. Make a note of the particular techniques that Frost uses to create his effects here.

Discussion

The range of techniques Frost uses in this poem includes:
* blank verse, used to convey the natural rhythms of speech as the narrator tells the tale
* simple, everyday language
* onomatopoeia, in the repeated phrase *snarled and rattled* (1, 7), creating an impression not only of the sound of the saw but also of its dangerous nature
* caesuras, to break the flow of the lines and interrupt the even pace; note how the caesuras become more marked and frequent after the accident, reflecting the way the routine rhythm of the farm work has been interrupted by the tragedy
* a detached narrator – the narrative voice seems emotionless and mostly objective
* the tempering of the narrator's objectivity with the brief expression of personal views, such as wishing the boy had been allowed to leave work earlier, and the comment that although doing *a man's work* he was *a child at heart* (24)
* personification, to create an impression of the saw coming to life and possessing unpredictable, dangerous and destructive powers
* the technique of the double shock, with first the accidental injury and then the unexpected death of the boy

- simple, realistic detail in creating a sense of the setting
- referring to the boy's family as *they*, which perhaps suggests a critical attitude towards them for not being more sensitive and more aware of the boy and his needs
- the use of exclamation marks to add emphasis at three key points in the poem: *But the hand!* (18), *Don't let him, sister!* (26), and *Little – less – nothing!* (32).

Form and style

We have seen that although Frost's poetry is often outwardly simple, its simplicity masks layers of meaning, and his poems can operate on many levels. Integral to the overall effects created by

Frost in 1962; the apparent simplicity of his poetry masks layers of meaning

the poems are a range of technical devices involving the use of form and structure, symbol and image, rhyme, rhythm and dramatic situation – all firmly embedded in the language of the poem.

Activity

Look at *Acquainted with the Night*. How does Frost make use of repetition and other techniques in this poem?

Discussion

The rhythm patterns created by the repetition of *I have*, together with the interlinking rhyme scheme, create a chant-like, incantatory effect that draws the reader into the poem, perhaps implying that the reader too will have experienced these feelings. Notice how Frost uses this repetition to develop and expand ideas, too – all three lines of the first stanza begin with *I have*, the first two of the second stanza, and just the first of the third stanza.

The metaphorical use of *night*, perhaps symbolizing depression or a sense of despair, is developed further through images such as *rain, light, a cry*. This sense of depression is heightened by lines such as *I have looked down the saddest city lane* (4) and *I have outwalked the furthest city light* (3), while *far away an interrupted cry* (8) again repeats the sense of pain and anguish, but also creates a sense of distance. The cry *Came over houses from another street,/ But not to call me back or say good-by* (9–10), again reinforcing the sense of loneliness and isolation. This feeling of distance is further emphasized by the lines:

And further still at unearthly height
One luminary clock against the sky

Proclaimed the time was neither wrong nor right.

(11–13)

The pattern of the poem creates a sense of an endless cycle through the repetition of the first line as the last line, perhaps reflecting the way in which depression can be self-perpetuating.

In some poems the rhyme scheme is a key element in the creation of tone.

Activity

How does Frost use rhyme in *The Cow in Apple Time*?

Discussion

The poem consists of 11 lines, the first eight of which are written in rhyming couplets. These lines describe a cow that has managed to get through or over a wall in order to get at fallen apples. The cow's pleasure in eating the apples is emphasized by the description of her: *Her face is flecked with pomace and she drools/ A cider syrup* (4–5).

Note how the caesura in line 5 marks the startling effect that the tempting apples have on the cow: *Having tasted fruit* (5) she is no longer interested in the pasture but *runs from tree to tree* to eat the sweet windfall apples.

Up to this point in the poem, the rhyme scheme, coupled with the rhythm of the lines, creates a light-hearted effect, presenting a humorous picture of the cow. This impression is reinforced through the speaker endowing the cow with thoughts – she *think[s] no more of wall-builders than fools* (3) and *scorns a pasture* (6) – and through the amusing visual imagery. However, in the final three lines the change to a triple rhyme alters the tone of the poem. The lightness of the earlier lines disappears and the amusing image of the cow is replaced by an image of decay, as the cow *bellows* (10) and *Her udder shrivels and the milk goes dry* (11).

The Cow in Apple Time is written in Frost's more usual decasyllabic (10-syllable) line, but he sometimes makes use of different forms too.

Activity

Compare the effects created by Frost's use of a shorter line in *The Sound of Trees* and *Neither Out Far nor In Deep*.

Discussion

The Sound of Trees opens with a question as the speaker ponders why we like the sound of trees *So close to our dwelling place* (5). The short lines, however, give an uneasy atmosphere to the poem, which reflects the tension the speaker feels between the sound of the trees which *We suffer* (6) and the effects they have:

> we lose all measure of pace,
> And fixity in our joys,
> And acquire a listening air.
>
> (7–9)

Notice that the speaker switches from first-person singular *I* to the plural in lines 2–9 to create a sense of inclusion and the idea that the comments apply to everyone, not only himself. He then switches back to the first-person singular to bring the description back to himself, the present situation, and the sense of his own isolation, before moving to the future tense for the conclusion of the poem. The final line is the shortest in the poem, and it brevity seems to give an added sense of finality to the language here.

In *Neither Out Far nor In Deep* Frost again makes use of a short line, in what Randall Jarrell (in *Poetry and the Age*, see Further Reading page 158) calls a 'very geometrical poem'. The apparently simple structure is reflected in the seemingly simple language, which has few descriptive terms and little imagery. However, Jarrell feels that the poem speaks to the reader through its structure rather than its language:

> First of all, of course, the poem is simply there, in different unchanging actuality; but our thoughts about it, what we are made to make of it, is there too, made to be there. When we choose between land and sea, the human and the inhuman, the finite and the infinite, the sea *has* to be the infinite that floods in over us endlessly, the hypnotic monotony of the universe that is incommensurable with us – everything into which we look neither very far nor very deep, but look, look just the same. And yet Frost doesn't say so – it's the geometry of this very geometrical poem, its inescapable structure, that says so.

The short, end-stopped lines are used here to create an emphasis that reinforces what some critics have seen as the sense of desolation evoked by a language that is stripped down to the minimum.

In the *The Ax-Helve* and *A Cabin in the Clearing*, Frost makes use of some unusual approaches.

Activity

Compare *The Ax-Helve* and *A Cabin in the Clearing*. What particularly strikes you about how Frost presents these poems, and what effects does he achieve?

Discussion

In *The Ax-Helve* Frost uses the image of the axe helve or handle to explore a variety of ideas. The poem is written in the form of a blank verse dramatic narrative. The speaker is interrupted while chopping wood by his neighbour, a Frenchman called Baptiste. He alerts the speaker to the fact that the axe helve he is using is of poor quality and promises him one of his own, handmade, good quality helves.

The story is told in Frost's usual narrative style, that of blank verse, but this poem is unusual because of his use of dialect form in the dialogue. This adds colour and realism to the character of Baptiste. Here he warns the narrator of the consequences of using a poor quality helve:

'You give her one good crack, she's snap raght off.
Den where's your hax-ead flying t'rough de hair?'

(26–27)

Baptiste invites the narrator to his house in order to give him a much better helve:

'Come on my house and I put you one in
What's las' awhile – good hick'ry what's grow crooked,
De second growt' I cut myself – tough, tough!'

(29–31)

Through the narrative Frost focuses on:

- human relationships, exploring how people attempt to create relationships while at the same time maintaining a degree of isolation – note the initial suspicion of the narrator as to Baptiste's motives
- neighbours and how they relate to each other – the narrator is unsure what Baptiste really wants and questions whether he is using the axe-helve *unscrupulously to bring me/ To see for once the inside of his house* (88–89)
- the idea of education, initiated through Baptiste's defence of why he has kept his children from school. This topic seems to have surprised the narrator and made him wonder what this has to do with axe-helves (82–87).

A Cabin in the Clearing is the title poem for Frost's final volume of poetry, *In the Clearing*. It is unusual in that the dialogue that takes place here between 'Smoke' and 'Mist' is in scripted form, and it is worth thinking about how this might affect the tone and impact of the poem. The poem is written in blank verse, through which Frost again creates a sense of natural dialogue between the personified 'Smoke' and 'Mist'.

Their dialogue centres around one of Frost's key themes, as the two discuss and reflect on the nature of the humans inhabiting the cabin and how, even though, as Smoke says, they have been there long enough *To push the woods back from around the house/ And part them in the middle with a path* (3–4), Mist still does not believe that they *know where they are* (5.)

Inside the cabin the inhabitants are restless as they grapple with the issues that concern us all, questions about who we are and why we are here – the *theme* of life:

> MIST. Listen, they murmur talking in the dark
> On what should be their daylong theme continued.
> Putting the lamp out has not put their thought out.
>
> (34–36)

Smoke does not despair for the human inhabitants of the cottage, however, and believes that they are capable of self-discovery. This idea that human beings spend much of their lives 'lost' is central to many of Frost's poems.

Here there is some hope, tenuous though it may be, expressed by
Smoke:

> If the day ever comes when they know who
> They are, they may know better where they are.

(29–30)

Critical views

Two of the striking features about the poetry of Robert Frost are
the wide appeal that it has had and how sustained his popularity
has been. Although he was 40 before he became widely known
and recognized as a poet, the popularity and acclaim that his
work attracted remained constant for the remaining 50 years of
his life, and has continued steadily since his death in 1963. He is
widely regarded as the most successful American poet and
throughout his long and distinguished career he had honour after
honour bestowed upon him, including winning the Pulitzer Prize
for Poetry four times (see pages 10–12). However, Frost is also a
poet who has polarized opinions about himself and his works in
a way that few poets have ever done.

On the one hand his admirers – a large and faithful following of
general readers – regard his poems as embodying quintessential
American values, including down-to-earth wisdom and a practical
view of life and the world, with self-reliance, an independence of
spirit and a strong sense of patriotism. This is achieved through a
voice that speaks to the reader in a straightforward way using clear,
simple and accessible language. He has also been admired by many
in the literary establishment for the very things that are missed by
those who see his poems as simple and straightforward. Critics have
recognized in his work a depth and complexity through which the
poems continually intrigue the reader by masking meanings and
requiring readers to work to discover interpretations for themselves.
This is one of the reasons why a reading that simply responds to the
surface meaning of the poem may often lead to a complete
misunderstanding of the poem and what Frost wanted to achieve.

147

His poems have also been admired for their technical accomplishments. Again, although superficially simple in structure and poetic technique they are, on closer examination, technically sophisticated, and make use of a wide range of stylistic techniques: imagery, metaphor, symbolism, rhyme, rhythm, metre, dramatic situation and voice. These features are often integrated in such a way that the reader only becomes aware of their full complexity and significance on closer analysis of the poem.

On the other hand, though, there were those who have felt 'that far from doing poetry a service by peddling his rustic charm and by bowing to the patriotic plaudits, Frost was in fact selling poetry disastrously short' (Ian Hamilton, see Further Reading page 157). The feeling was that often the popular acclaim had more to do with the image that Frost had created for himself than the work itself, and those poets who did not display his image of no-nonsense true Americanism were either criticized through comparison or ignored. As Hamilton points out:

> These two ways of viewing Frost remained fairly constantly in evidence throughout his career – on the one hand, the popular idol, on the other the object of suspicion and some bitterness in the eyes of a highbrow-radical literary world.

Although these views remained largely unchanged after Frost's death in 1963, in 1970 the publication of Frost's official biography by Lawrance Thompson caused a stir among both the critics and the general admirers of his work. Rather surprisingly, particularly as Thompson had been appointed by Frost as his official biographer, in the second volume of the biography, *Robert Frost: The Years of Triumph: 1915–1938*, he presents a picture of Frost as a man with many negative qualities. Thompson draws attention to the vanity, jealousy and vindictiveness of a man who, throughout his life, created, promoted and sustained the image of himself he wanted the public to see.

However, these revelations, although making it impossible to view Frost the poet in quite the same way again, did allow for a re-evaluation of his work, such as that presented by Pritchard's

Frost: A Literary Life Reconsidered (see Further Reading). Such re-evaluations have made it much more possible to separate Frost's work from his life, which is a useful corrective as some interpretations have relied too heavily on biographical detail as a way of explaining the 'meaning' of his poetry. There has been much more recognition that his poems, rather than being cosy and comforting, and although they reinforce positive values, are, as Hamilton says, 'much more negative than positive'. Many contain the quality that the critic Lionel Trilling termed 'terrifying' in the sense of futility and desperation that lies beneath the words.

There is little doubt that Frost did much to create his own image through his many public performances, poetry readings, lectures and appearances, but in the end, as Warren Hope (see Further Reading) puts it:

> Those people who have come to think of Frost as a nasty man who wrote terrifying poems are probably as far from the mark as those who thought of him as an avuncular duffer who wrote quaint lyrics. He was a man, not a caricature – not even the caricature of his own making, the stage Yankee with the craggy brows.

Frost in old age with his dog; the popularity of his poems has endured

Essay Questions

1 'Good fences make good neighbours.' Do you think this sums up the message that Frost wanted to convey in *Mending Wall*? Explore your interpretations of the poem.

2 Compare the ways in which Frost uses images of leaves as a metaphor to explore his ideas in *A Leaf-Treader*, *In Hardwood Groves* and *Gathering Leaves*.

3 Discuss the ways in which nature is significant in *The Tuft of Flowers*, and how this poem relates to other poems by Frost you have studied. Explore the effects created by Frost's use of language, imagery and viewpoint in these poems.

4 Compare the ways in which Frost explores his ideas in *Ghost House* and *Waiting*. In your answer you should look closely at the poet's use of language and the effects created.

5 Examine the ways in which Frost explores ideas about loneliness and isolation in three poems you have studied.

6 Explore the ways in which Frost presents narratives in *Home Burial* and *The Black Cottage*.

7 Do you see *The Oven Bird* as a pessimistic or celebratory poem? Compare the ideas Frost expresses here with those in two other poems you have studied.

8 How does Frost use the image of snow to explore his ideas in *Desert Places* and *Stopping by Woods on a Snowy Evening*? In your answer you should examine closely Frost's use of language to achieve his effects.

9 Discuss the ways in which Frost uses activities or events to do with farming as the starting point to explore ideas about life in three of the poems you have studied. In your response you should examine the effects created by Frost's use of language, imagery and viewpoint.

10 Compare the ways in which Frost uses an encounter with the natural in *Two Look at Two* and one other Frost poem you have studied. Explore the ideas Frost presents in the poems and the ways in which he achieves his effects.

11 Compare Frost's use of humour in *An Unstamped Letter in Our Rural Letter Box* and one other poem you have studied. You should discuss the effects created through language and style as well as the ideas in the poems.

12 How does Frost create a disturbing and unsettling atmosphere in *The Draft Horse*? Compare the effect created here with a similar disturbing effect created in one other poem by Frost that you have studied.

13 Explore the ways in which the use of rhyme and structure in Frost's poetry is important to the overall effectiveness of the poems. You should base your answer on three poems you have studied.

14 Compare the ways in which Frost uses narrative voice in *The Ax-Helve* and *A Cabin in the Clearing*.

15 Choose three poems you have studied in which Frost uses trees as an image to explore his ideas on life. Compare the ways in which he uses language, imagery and form in these poems to create his effects and develop his thoughts.

16 In the light of your study of Frost's poetry, how far do you think that the ideas expressed in *The Most of It* and *There Are Roughly Zones* are representative of his philosophy of life?

17 Examine the ways in which Frost uses symbols in his poetry. You should focus on a detailed analysis of two or three poems in your answer.

18 How does Frost explore the idea of human limitation in *The Middleness of the Road* and one or two other poems you have studied?

19 In what ways is the idea of the cycle of life important in Frost's poetry? In your response you should analyse in detail three poems you have studied.

20 Frost wanted to use everyday language in his poetry, a language he described as 'absolutely unliterary'. In the light of your study of Frost's poetry, how far do you think he has achieved this end? You should focus on details of language and stylistic features from the poems to support and illustrate your ideas.

Chronology

1874 Robert Frost born in San Francisco

1885 Death of his father, William Frost; family moves to Massachusetts

1891 Meets his future wife, Elinor, at school

1892 Enrols at Dartmouth College, but leaves within a year

1894 *My Butterfly: An Elegy* published in *The Independent*, New York

1895 Marries Elinor

1896 Birth of first son, Elliott

1897 Begins classes at Harvard University

1899 Leaves Harvard without completing his course; tries chicken farming

1900 Death of Elliott; death of his mother, Isabelle

1901 Frost's uncle helps him to purchase a farm at Derry, New Hampshire

1906 Begins teaching at Pinkerton Academy

1911 Sells the farm and begins teaching at Plymouth State Normal School

1912 Sails to England with his family

1913 *A Boy's Will* published; meets Ezra Pound, Georgian poets and Edward Thomas

1914 Moves to Dymock, Gloucestershire, with his family; outbreak of First World War

1915 *North of Boston* published; returns to US; buys a farm in New Hampshire

1916 *Mountain Interval* published

1917 Begins teaching at Amherst College

1920 Leaves Amherst; moves to Vermont

1921 Takes up teaching post in Michigan

1923   Resigns teaching post in Michigan; returns to
       Amherst College; *Selected Poems* published; *New
       Hampshire* published
1924   Awarded Pulitzer Prize for *New Hampshire*
1925   Resigns from Amherst College; returns to
       Michigan
1926   Leaves Michigan and returns to Amherst
       (until 1938)
1928   Revisits Europe; renews acquaintance with the
       Dymock poets; *West-Running Brook* published
1930   *Collected Poems* published; wins second
       Pulitzer Prize
1934   Death of his youngest (and favourite) daughter,
       Marjorie, aged 29
1936   A *Further Range* published
1937   Awarded third Pulitzer Prize
1938   Death of his wife, Elinor
1939   Fellowship in Poetry at Harvard University
       (until 1941)
1940   Suicide of his son, Carol, aged 38
1942   A *Witness Tree* published; wins fourth Pulitzer
       Prize
1943   Fellowship at Dartmouth College (until 1949)
1947   *Steeple Bush* published
1949   Final return to Amherst College (until 1954)
1957   Visits England to receive honorary degrees at
       Durham, Oxford and Cambridge; lectures in
       London; final visit to Dymock
1961   Takes part in inauguration of President Kennedy
1962   *In the Clearing* published; visits Russia and meets
       Prime Minister Khrushchev as an American
       cultural ambassador just before the Cuban
       Missile Crisis
1963   Dies, 29 January

Further Reading

Editions

Ian Hamilton (ed.), *Robert Frost: Selected Poems* (Penguin, 1973)

Edward Connery Lathem (ed.), *The Poetry of Robert Frost* (Jonathan Cape, 1971)

Edward Connery Lathem and Lawrance Thompson (eds.), *Robert Frost: Poetry and Prose* (Holt, Rinehart and Winston, Inc., 1972)

Richard Poirier and Mark Richardson (eds.), *Collected Poems, Plays and Prose by Robert Frost* (Library of America, 1995)

Lawrance Thompson (ed.), *Selected Letters of Robert Frost* (Holt, Rinehart and Winston, Inc., 1964)

Biography

Jeffrey Meyers, *Robert Frost: A Biography* (Constable, 1996)

William H. Pritchard, *Frost: A Literary Life Reconsidered* (University of Massachusetts Press, 2nd ed., 1993)

Lawrance Thompson, *Robert Frost: The Early Years, 1874–1915* (Holt, 1966)

Lawrance Thompson, *Robert Frost: The Years of Triumph, 1915–1938* (Holt, 1970)

Lawrance Thompson and R.H. Winnick, *Robert Frost: The Later Years, 1938–1963* (Holt, 1976)

Lawrance Thompson and R.H. Winnick, *Robert Frost: A Biography* (Holt, Rinehart and Winston, Inc., 1981)

John Walsh, *Into My Own: The English Years of Robert Frost* (Grove Press, 1988)

Criticism

Harold Bloom, ed., *Robert Frost* (Chelsea House Publications, 1998)

Joseph Brodsky, Seamus Heaney, and Derek Walcott, *Homage to Robert Frost* (Faber and Faber, 1997)

Reginald Cook, *The Dimensions of Robert Frost* (Rinehart and Co., Inc., 1958)

Warren Hope, *Student Guide to Robert Frost* (Greenwich Exchange, 2004)

Randall Jarrell, 'To the Laodiceans' in *Poetry and the Age* (Vintage, 1955)

Judith Oster, *Toward Robert Frost: The Reader and the Poet* (University of Georgia Press, 1991)

Richard Poirier, *Robert Frost: The Work of Knowing* (Stanford University Press, revised ed. 1990)

CD

Joe Matazzoni and Donald Sheehy (eds.), *Robert Frost: Poems, Life, Legacy* (Henry Holt, 1997). This interactive CD-Rom contains video and audio recordings of Frost, complete text of his poems, interviews, biographical and critical studies.

Index of Titles and First Lines